PRESENTED TO: _Danielle Hickman_

FROM: _Calvary Baptist_

DATE: _May 17, 2015_

GROWING
IN
GRACE

Published by Worthy Inspired, a division of Worthy Media, Inc.,
134 Franklin Road, Suite 200, Brentwood, Tennessee 37027.

Scripture references marked KJV are from the Holy Bible, King James Version.

Scripture references marked NKJV are from the Holy Bible, New King James Version. Copyright © 1982 by Thomas Nelson, Inc. Used by permission.

Scripture references marked NCV are from the New Century Version®. Copyright © 1987, 1988, 1991 by Word Publishing, a division of Thomas Nelson, Inc. All rights reserved. Used by permission.

Scripture references marked HCSB are from the Holman Christian Standard Bible™ Copyright © 1999, 2000, 2001 by Holman Bible Publishers. Used by permission.

Scripture references marked NIV are from the Holy Bible, New International Version®. Copyright © 1973, 1978, 1984 International Bible Society. Used by permission of Zondervan. All rights reserved.

Scripture references marked NLT are from the Holy Bible. New Living Translation. Copyright © 1996 Tyndale Charitable Trust. Used by permission of Tyndale House Publishers.

Scripture references marked TLB are from the Holy Bible, The Living Bible, Copyright © 1971 owned by assignment by Illinois Regional Bank N.A. (as trustee). Used by permission of Tyndale House Publishers, Inc., Wheaton, Illinois 60189. All rights reserved.

Scripture references marked NASB are from the New American Standard Bible®. Copyright © 1960, 1962, 1963, 1968, 1971, 1972, 1973, 1975, 1977, 1995 by The Lockman Foundation. Used by permission.

Scripture references marked MSG are from the Message. Copyright © 1993, 1994, 1995, 1996, 2000, 2001, 2002. Used by permission of NavPress Publishing Group.

Cover Design by Kim Russell / Wahoo Designs
Page Layout by Bart Dawson

Printed in China

1 2 3 4 5—RRD—18 17 16 15 14

GROWING
IN
GRACE

WORTHY
Inspired

INTRODUCTION

How desperately our world needs Christian women who are willing to honor God with their praise, their prayers, and their service. Hopefully, you are determined to become such a woman—a woman who walks in wisdom as she offers counsel and direction to her family, to her friends, and to her coworkers.

This generation faces problems that defy easy solutions, yet face them we must. We need women whose vision is clear and whose intentions are pure. And this book can help.

In your hands, you hold a book that contains 100 devotional readings that are intended to remind you of God's love and God's grace. During the next 100 days, please try this experiment: read a chapter each day. If you're already committed to a daily worship time, this book will enrich that experience. If you are not, the simple act of giving God a few minutes each morning will change the direction and the quality of your life.

As you consider your own circumstances, remember this: whatever the size of your challenge, whatever the scope of your problem, God is bigger. Much bigger. He will instruct you, protect you, energize you, and heal you if you let Him. So let Him. Pray fervently, listen carefully, work diligently, and treat every single day as an opportunity for praise and worship because that's precisely what every day can be . . . and should be.

FOR BY GRACE
YOU ARE SAVED THROUGH
FAITH, AND THIS IS
NOT FROM YOURSELVES;
IT IS GOD'S GIFT—
NOT FROM WORKS,
SO THAT NO ONE CAN BOAST.

—

Ephesians 2:8-9 HCSB

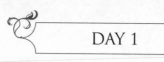

THE GIFT OF GRACE

For all have sinned, and fall short of the glory of God, being justified freely by His grace through the redemption that is in Christ Jesus....

—Romans 3:23-24 NKJV

Romans 3:23 reminds us that all of us fall short of the glory of God. Yet despite our imperfections and despite our shortcomings, He sent His Son so that we might be redeemed from our sins. In doing so, God showed His infinite mercy and His infinite love.

We have received countless gifts from God, but none can compare with the gift of salvation. God's grace is the ultimate gift, and we owe Him the ultimate in thanksgiving. Let us praise the Creator for His priceless gift, and let us share the Good News with our families, with our friends, and with the world.

Christ sacrificed His life on the cross so that we might have eternal life. This gift, freely given from God's only begotten Son, is the priceless possession of everyone who accepts Him as Lord and Savior. We return His love by welcoming Him into our hearts and sharing His message and His love. When we do so, we are blessed here on earth and throughout all eternity.

You're about to begin a 100-day journey, an exploration of your faith: what it is at this moment, what it should be today, and what it can become tomorrow. During the next 100 days, you will be challenged to examine your thoughts, your priorities, your habits, and your behaviors. And you'll be challenged to strengthen your faith by learning to trust God more every day.

The Christian life is motivated not by a list of do's and don'ts, but by the gracious outpouring of God's love and blessing.

Anne Graham Lotz

A PRAYER FOR GRACE

Dear Lord, You have offered Your grace freely through Christ Jesus. I praise You for that priceless gift. Let me share the good news of Your Son with a world that desperately needs His peace, His abundance, His love, and His salvation. Amen

EXPERIENCING CHRIST'S LOVE

For I am persuaded that neither death nor life, nor angels nor principalities nor powers, nor things present nor things to come, nor height nor depth, nor any other created thing, shall be able to separate us from the love of God which is in Christ Jesus our Lord.

—Romans 8:38-39 NKJV

How much does Christ love us? More than we, as mere mortals, can comprehend. His love is perfect and steadfast. Even though we are fallible and wayward, the Good Shepherd cares for us still. Even though we have fallen far short of the Father's commandments, Christ loves us with a power and depth that are beyond our understanding. The sacrifice that Jesus made upon the cross was made for each of us, and His love endures to the edge of eternity and beyond.

Christ is the ultimate Savior of mankind and the personal Savior of those who believe in Him.

As His servants, we should place Him at the very center of our lives. And, every day that God gives us breath, we should share Christ's love and His message with a world that needs both.

Christ's love changes everything. When you accept His gift of grace, you are transformed, not only for today, but also for all eternity. If you haven't already done so, accept Jesus Christ as your Savior. He's waiting patiently for you to invite Him into your heart. Please don't make Him wait a single minute longer.

It is when we come to the Lord in our nothingness, our powerlessness and our helplessness that He then enables us to love in a way which, without Him, would be absolutely impossible.

Elisabeth Elliot

A PRAYER FOR GRACE

Dear Jesus, I praise You for Your love, a love that never ends. Today, I will return Your love and I will share it with the world. Amen

PRAISE HIM AND THANK HIM

*And whatever you do, in word or in deed, do
everything in the name of the Lord Jesus, giving
thanks to God the Father through Him.*

—Colossians 3:17 HCSB

Sometimes, life-here-on-earth can be complicated, demanding, and busy. When the demands of life leave us rushing from place to place with scarcely a moment to spare, we may fail to pause and say a word of thanks for all the good things we've received. But when we fail to count our blessings, we rob ourselves of the happiness, the peace, and the gratitude that should rightfully be ours.

Today, even if you're busily engaged in life, slow down long enough to start counting your blessings. You most certainly will not be able to count them all, but take a few moments to jot down as many blessings as you can. Then, give thanks to the Giver of all good things: God.

His love for you is eternal, as are His gifts. And it's never too soon—or too late—to offer Him thanks.

Thanksgiving or complaining—these words express two contrastive attitudes of the souls of God's children in regard to His dealings with them. The soul that gives thanks can find comfort in everything; the soul that complains can find comfort in nothing.

Hannah Whitall Smith

A PRAYER FOR GRACE

Heavenly Father, Your gifts are greater than I can imagine. May I live each day with thanksgiving in my heart and praise on my lips. Thank You for the gift of Your Son and for the promise of eternal life. Let me share the joyous news of Jesus Christ, and let my life be a testimony to His love and His grace. Amen

DAY 4

SERVE HIM

We must do the works of Him who sent Me while it is day. Night is coming when no one can work.

—John 9:4 HCSB

The teachings of Jesus are clear: We achieve greatness through service to others. But, as weak human beings, we sometimes fall short as we seek to puff ourselves up and glorify our own accomplishments. Jesus commands otherwise. He teaches us that the most esteemed men and women are not the self-congratulatory leaders of society but are instead the humblest of servants.

Today, you may feel the temptation to build yourself up in the eyes of your neighbors. Resist that temptation. Instead, serve your neighbors quietly and without fanfare. Find a need and fill it . . . humbly. Lend a helping hand and share a word of kindness . . . anonymously, for this is God's way.

As a humble servant, you will glorify yourself not before men, but before God, and that's what

God intends. After all, earthly glory is fleeting: here today and all too soon gone. But, heavenly glory endures throughout eternity. So, the choice is yours: Either you can lift yourself up here on earth and be humbled in heaven, or vice versa. Choose vice versa.

God wants us to serve Him with a willing spirit, one that would choose no other way.

Beth Moore

A PRAYER FOR GRACE

Dear Lord, in weak moments, I seek to build myself up by placing myself ahead of others. But Your commandment, Father, is that I become a humble servant to those who need my encouragement, my help, and my love. Create in me a servant's heart. And, let be a woman who follows in the footsteps of Your Son Jesus who taught us by example that to be great in Your eyes, Lord, is to serve others humbly, faithfully, and lovingly. Amen

FINDING GENUINE PEACE

But now in Christ Jesus you who once were far off have been brought near by the blood of Christ. For He Himself is our peace.

—Ephesians 2:13-14 NKJV

On many occasions, our outer struggles are simply manifestations of the inner conflicts that we feel when we stray from God's path. What's needed is a refresher course in God's promise of peace. The beautiful words of John 14:27 remind us that Jesus offers peace, not as the world gives, but as He alone gives: "Peace I leave with you. My peace I give to you. I do not give to you as the world gives. Your heart must not be troubled or fearful" (HCSB).

As believers, our challenge is straightforward: we should welcome Christ's peace into our hearts and then, as best we can, share His peace with our neighbors.

Today, as a gift to yourself, to your family, and to your friends, invite Christ to preside over every aspect of your life. It's the best way to live and the surest path to peace . . . today and forever.

To know God as He really is—in His essential nature and character—is to arrive at a citadel of peace that circumstances may storm, but can never capture.

Catherine Marshall

Prayer guards hearts and minds and causes God to bring peace out of chaos.

Beth Moore

A PRAYER FOR GRACE

Dear Lord, let me accept the peace and abundance that You offer through Your Son Jesus. You are the Giver of all things good, Father, and You give me peace when I draw close to You. Help me to trust Your will, to follow Your commands, and to accept Your peace, today and forever. Amen

ASK HIM

Keep asking, and it will be given to you. Keep searching, and you will find. Keep knocking, and the door will be opened to you. For everyone who asks receives, and the one who searches finds, and to the one who knocks, the door will be opened.

—Matthew 7:7-8 HCSB

Are you a woman who confidently asks God to move mountains, or do you timidly ask Him to push around a few molehills? God is perfectly capable of moving either molehills or mountains, so it's up to you to decide whether you want His help on big projects or tiny ones.

How often do you ask for God's help? Occasionally? Intermittently? Whenever you experience a crisis? Hopefully not. Hopefully, you have developed the habit of asking for God's assistance early and often. And hopefully, you have learned to seek His guidance in every aspect of your life.

God has promised that when you ask for His help, He will not withhold it. So ask. Ask Him to meet the needs of your day. Ask Him for wisdom. Ask Him to lead you, to protect you, and to correct you. And don't hesitate to ask Him to do big things in your own life and in the lives of your loved ones.

God stands at the door and waits. When you knock on His door, He answers. Your task, of course, is to seek His guidance prayerfully, confidently, and often.

God uses our most stumbling, faltering faith-steps as the open door to His doing for us "more than we ask or think."

Catherine Marshall

A PRAYER FOR GRACE

Lord, when I have questions or fears, I will turn to You. When I am weak, I will seek Your strength. When I am discouraged, Father, I will be mindful of Your love and Your grace. I will ask You for the things I need, Father, and I will trust Your answers, today and forever. Amen

TRUST GOD'S PROMISES

This is my comfort in my affliction: Your promise has given me life.

—Psalm 119:50 HCSB

God's promises are found in a book like no other: the Holy Bible. The Bible is a roadmap for life here on earth and for life eternal. As Christians, we are called upon to trust its promises, to follow its commandments, and to share its Good News.

As believers, we must study the Bible daily and meditate upon its meaning for our lives. Otherwise, we deprive ourselves of a priceless gift from our Creator. God's Holy Word is, indeed, a transforming, life-changing, one-of-a-kind treasure. And, a passing acquaintance with the Good Book is insufficient for Christians who seek to obey God's Word and to understand His will.

God has made promises to mankind and to you. God's promises never fail and they never grow old. You must trust those promises and share them with your family, with your friends, and with the world.

Fear and doubt are conquered by a faith that rejoices. And faith can rejoice because the promises of God are as certain as God Himself.

Kay Arthur

We have ample evidence that the Lord is able to guide. The promises cover every imaginable situation. All we need to do is to take the hand he stretches out.

Elisabeth Elliot

A PRAYER FOR GRACE

Lord, Your Holy Word contains promises, and I will trust them. I will use the Bible as my guide, and I will trust You, Lord, to speak to me through Your Holy Spirit and through Your Holy Word, this day and forever. Amen

GUARD YOUR HEART AND MIND

Guard your heart above all else, for it is the source of life.

—Proverbs 4:23 HCSB

You are near and dear to God. He loves you more than you can imagine, and He wants the very best for you. And one more thing: God wants you to guard your heart.

Every day, you are faced with choices . . . more choices than you can count. You can do the right thing, or not. You can be prudent, or not. You can be kind, and generous, and obedient to God. Or not.

Today, the world will offer you countless opportunities to let down your guard and, by doing so, make needless mistakes that may injure you or your loved ones. So be watchful and obedient. Guard your heart by giving it to your Heavenly Father; it is safe with Him.

Holiness has never been the driving force of the majority. It is, however, mandatory for anyone who wants to enter the kingdom.

Elisabeth Elliot

He doesn't need an abundance of words. He doesn't need a dissertation about your life. He just wants your attention. He wants your heart.

Kathy Troccoli

If all struggles and sufferings were eliminated, the spirit would no more reach maturity than would the child.

Elisabeth Elliot

A PRAYER FOR GRACE

Dear Lord, I will guard my heart against the evils, the temptations, and the distractions of this world. I will focus, instead, upon Your love, Your blessings, and Your Son. Amen

LIVING WITH YOUR BELIEFS

For the kingdom of God is not in talk but in power.

—1 Corinthians 4:20 HCSB

In describing our beliefs, our actions are far better descriptors than our words. Yet far too many of us spend more energy talking about our beliefs than living by them—with predictably poor results.

As believers, we must beware: Our actions should always give credence to the changes that Christ can make in the lives of those who walk with Him.

Your beliefs shape your values, and your values shape your life. Is your life a clearly crafted picture book of your creed? And do you weave your beliefs into the very fabric of your day. If you do, God will honor your good works, and your good works will honor God.

If you seek to be a responsible believer, you must realize that it is never enough to hear the instructions of God; you must also live by them.

And it is never enough to wait idly by while others do God's work here on earth. You, too, must act.

Doing God's work is a responsibility that every Christian (including you) should bear. And when you do, your loving Heavenly Father will reward your efforts with a bountiful harvest.

Jesus taught that the evidence that confirms our leaps of faith comes after we risk believing, not before.

Gloria Gaither

God has power and He's willing to share it if we step out in faith and believe that He will.

Bill Hybels

A PRAYER FOR GRACE

Heavenly Father, I believe in You, and I believe in Your Word. Help me to live in such a way that my actions validate my beliefs—and let the glory be Yours forever. Amen

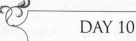

SPIRITUAL GROWTH

Therefore, leaving the elementary message about the Messiah, let us go on to maturity.

—Hebrews 6:1 HCSB

Are you continuing to grow in your love and knowledge of the Lord, or are you "satisfied" with the current state of your spiritual health? Your relationship with God is ongoing; it unfolds day by day, and it offers countless opportunities to grow closer to Him . . . or not. As each new day unfolds, you are confronted with a wide range of decisions: how you will behave, where you will direct your thoughts, with whom you will associate, and what you will choose to worship. These choices, along with many others like them, are yours and yours alone. How you choose determines how your relationship with God will unfold.

Hopefully, you're determined to make yourself a growing Christian. Your Savior deserves no less, and neither, by the way, do you.

We set our eyes on the finish line, forgetting the past, and straining toward the mark of spiritual maturity and fruitfulness.

Vonette Bright

You are either becoming more like Christ every day or you're becoming less like Him. There is no neutral position in the Lord.

Stormie Omartian

If all struggles and sufferings were eliminated, the spirit would no more reach maturity than would the child.

Elisabeth Elliot

A PRAYER FOR GRACE

Dear Lord, thank You for the opportunity to walk with Your Son. And, thank You for the opportunity to grow closer to You each day. I thank You for the person I am . . . and for the person I can become. Amen

HIS GRACE IS SUFFICIENT FOR DIFFICULT DAYS

We are troubled on every side, yet not distressed; we are perplexed, but not in despair....

—2 Corinthians 4:8 KJV

A s we travel the roads of life, all of us are confronted with streets that seem to be dead ends. When we do, we may become discouraged. After all, we live in a society where expectations can be high and demands even higher.

If you find yourself enduring difficult circumstances, remember that God remains in His heaven. If you become discouraged with the direction of your day or your life, turn your thoughts and prayers to Him. He is a God of possibility, not negativity. He will guide you through your difficulties and beyond them. And then, with a renewed spirit of optimism and hope, you can thank the Giver of all things good for gifts that are simply too profound to fully understand and for treasures that are too numerous to count.

If God sends us on stony paths, he provides strong shoes.

Corrie ten Boom

We all go through pain and sorrow, but the presence of God, like a warm, comforting blanket, can shield us and protect us, and allow the deep inner joy to surface, even in the most devastating circumstances.

Barbara Johnson

A PRAYER FOR GRACE

Heavenly Father, You are my strength and my refuge. As I journey through this day, I know that I may encounter disappointments and losses. When I am troubled, let me turn to You. Keep me steady, Lord, and renew a right spirit inside of me this day and forever. Amen

DREAMING
BIG DREAMS

When dreams come true, there is life and joy.

—Proverbs 13:12 NLT

Are you willing to entertain the possibility that God has big plans in store for you? Hopefully so. Yet sometimes, especially if you've recently experienced a life-altering disappointment, you may find it difficult to envision a brighter future for yourself and your family. If so, it's time to reconsider your own capabilities . . . and God's.

Your Heavenly Father created you with unique gifts and untapped talents; your job is to tap them. When you do, you'll begin to feel an increasing sense of confidence in yourself and in your future.

It takes courage to dream big dreams. You will discover that courage when you do three things: accept the past, trust God to handle the future, and make the most of the time He has given you today.

Nothing is too difficult for God, and no dreams are too big for Him—not even yours. So start living—and dreaming—accordingly.

Always stay connected to people and seek out things that bring you joy. Dream with abandon. Pray confidently.

Barbara Johnson

Set goals so big that unless God helps you, you will be a miserable failure.

Bill Bright

A PRAYER FOR GRACE

Dear Lord, give me the courage to dream and the faithfulness to trust in Your perfect plan. When I am worried or weary, give me strength for today and hope for tomorrow. Keep me mindful of Your healing power, Your infinite love, and Your eternal salvation. Amen

MAKING THE MOST OF YOUR TALENTS

I remind you to keep ablaze the gift of God that is in you.

—2 Timothy 1:6 HCSB

Your talents, resources, and opportunities are all gifts from the Giver of all things good. And the best way to say "Thank You" for these gifts is to use them.

Do you have a particular talent? Hone your skill and use it. Do you possess financial resources? Share them. Have you been blessed by a particular opportunity, or have you experienced unusual good fortune? Use your good fortune to help others.

When you share the gifts God has given you—and when you share them freely and without fanfare—you invite God to bless you more and more. So today, do yourself and the world a favor: be a faithful steward of your talents and treasures. And then prepare yourself for even greater blessings that are sure to come.

God often reveals His direction for our lives through the way He made us, with a certain personality and unique skills.

Bill Hybels

Employ whatever God has entrusted you with, in doing good, all possible good, in every possible kind and degree.

John Wesley

What we are is God's gift to us. What we become is our gift to God.

Anonymous

A PRAYER FOR GRACE

Father, You have given me abilities to be used for the glory of Your kingdom. Give me the courage and the perseverance to use those talents. Keep me mindful that all my gifts come from You, Lord. Let me be Your faithful, humble servant, and let me give You all the glory and all the praise. Amen

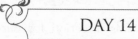

THE IMPORTANCE OF CHEERFULNESS

Be cheerful. Keep things in good repair. Keep your spirits up. Think in harmony. Be agreeable. Do all that, and the God of love and peace will be with you for sure.

—2 Corinthians 13:11 MSG

On some days, as every woman knows, it's hard to be cheerful. Sometimes, as the demands of the world increase and our energy sags, we feel less like "cheering up" and more like "tearing up." But even in our darkest hours, we can turn to God, and He will give us comfort.

Few things in life are more sad, or, for that matter, more absurd, than a grumpy Christian. Christ promises us lives of abundance and joy, but He does not force His joy upon us. We must claim His joy for ourselves, and when we do, Jesus, in turn, fills our spirits with His power and His love.

How can we receive from Christ the joy that is rightfully ours? By giving Him what is rightfully His: our hearts and our souls.

When we earnestly commit ourselves to the Savior of mankind, when we place Jesus at the center of our lives and trust Him as our personal Savior, He will transform us, not just for today, but for all eternity. Then we, as God's children, can share Christ's joy and His message with a world that needs both.

God is good, and heaven is forever. And if those two facts don't cheer you up, nothing will.

Marie T. Freeman

A PRAYER FOR GRACE

Dear Lord, You have given me so many reasons to celebrate. Today, let me choose an attitude of cheerfulness. Let me be a joyful Christian, Lord, quick to smile and slow to anger. And, let me share Your goodness with all whom I meet so that Your love might shine in me and through me. Amen

YOUR OWN WORST CRITIC?

For You have made him a little lower than the angels, and You have crowned him with glory and honor.

—Psalm 8:5 NKJV

Are you your own worst critic? If so, it's time to become a little more understanding of the woman you see whenever you look into the mirror.

Millions of words have been written about various ways to improve self-image and increase self-esteem. Yet, maintaining a healthy self-image is, to a surprising extent, a matter of doing three things: 1. behaving yourself 2. thinking healthy thoughts 3. finding a purpose for your life that pleases your Creator and yourself.

The Bible affirms the importance of self-acceptance by teaching Christians to love others as they love themselves (Matthew 22:37-40). God accepts us just as we are. And, if He accepts us—faults and all—then who are we to believe otherwise?

Being loved by Him whose opinion matters most gives us the security to risk loving, too—even loving ourselves.

Gloria Gaither

If you ever put a price tag on yourself, it would have to read "Jesus" because that is what God paid to save you.

Josh McDowell

A PRAYER FOR GRACE

Lord, I have so much to learn and so many ways to improve myself, but You love me just as I am. Thank You for Your love and for Your Son. And, help me to become the person that You want me to become. Amen

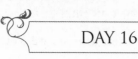

TRUSTING YOUR CONSCIENCE

Now the goal of our instruction is love from a pure heart, a good conscience, and a sincere faith.

—1 Timothy 1:5 HCSB

Few things in life torment us more than a guilty conscience. And, few things in life provide more contentment than the knowledge that we are obeying God's commandments. A clear conscience is one of the rewards we earn when we obey God's Word and follow His will. When we follow God's will and accept His gift of salvation, our earthly rewards are never-ceasing, and our heavenly rewards are everlasting.

Billy Graham correctly observed, "Most of us follow our conscience as we follow a wheelbarrow. We push it in front of us in the direction we want to go." If that describes you, then here's a word of warning: both you and your wheelbarrow are headed for trouble.

You can sometimes keep secrets from other people, but you can never keep secrets from God.

God knows what you think and what you do. And if you want to please Him, you must start with good intentions, a pure heart, and a clear conscience.

If you sincerely wish to walk with God, follow His commandments. When you do, your character will take care of itself . . . and so will your conscience. Then, as you journey through life, you won't need to look over your shoulder to see who—besides God—is watching.

It is neither safe nor prudent to do anything against one's conscience.

Martin Luther

A PRAYER FOR GRACE

Dear Lord, You speak to me through the gift of Your Holy Word. And, Father, You speak to me through that still small voice that tells me right from wrong. Let me follow Your way, Lord, and, in these quiet moments, show me Your plan for this day, that I might serve You. Amen

FINDING CONTENTMENT

But godliness with contentment is a great gain.

—1 Timothy 6:6 HCSB

Everywhere we turn, or so it seems, the world promises us contentment and happiness. We are bombarded by messages for the media offering us the "good life" if only we will purchase products and services that are designed to provide happiness, success, and contentment. But the contentment that the world offers is fleeting and incomplete. Thankfully, the contentment that God offers is all encompassing and everlasting.

Happiness depends less upon our circumstances than upon our thoughts. When we turn our thoughts to God, to His gifts, and to His glorious creation, we experience the joy that God intends for His children. But, when we focus on the negative aspects of life—or when we disobey God's commandments—we cause ourselves needless suffering.

Do you sincerely want to be a contented Christian? Then set your mind and your heart upon God's love and His grace. Seek first the salvation that is available through a personal relationship with Jesus Christ, and then claim the joy, the contentment, and the spiritual abundance that God offers His children.

The key to contentment is to consider. Consider who you are and be satisfied with that. Consider what you have and be satisfied with that. Consider what God's doing and be satisfied with that.

Luci Swindoll

A PRAYER FOR GRACE

Dear Lord, You offer me contentment, and I praise You for that gift. Today, I will accept Your peace. I will trust Your Word, I will follow Your commandments, and I will welcome the peace of Jesus into my heart, today and forever. Amen

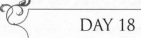
STRENGTH FOR TODAY

Search for the Lord and for His strength; seek His face always.

—Psalm 105:4-5 HCSB

God's love and support never changes. From the cradle to the grave, God has promised to give you the strength to meet any challenge. God has promised to lift you up and guide your steps if you let Him. God has promised that when you entrust your life to Him completely and without reservation, He will give you the courage to face any trial and the wisdom to live in His righteousness.

God's hand uplifts those who turn their hearts and prayers to Him. Will you count yourself among that number? Will you accept God's peace and wear God's armor against the temptations and distractions of our dangerous world? If you do, you can live courageously and optimistically, knowing that you have been forever touched by the loving, unfailing, uplifting hand of God.

The miraculous thing about being a family is that in the last analysis, we are each dependent of one another and God, woven together by mercy given and mercy received.

Barbara Johnson

No matter how heavy the burden, daily strength is given, so I expect we need not give ourselves any concern as to what the outcome will be. We must simply go forward.

Annie Armstrong

When we spend time with Christ, He supplies us with strength and encourages us in the pursuit of His ways.

Elizabeth George

A PRAYER FOR GRACE

Dear Lord, I will turn to You for strength. When my responsibilities seem overwhelming, I will trust You to give me courage and perspective. Today and every day, I will look to You as the ultimate source of my hope, my strength, my peace, and my salvation. Amen

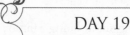

DEFINING SUCCESS

*If you do not stand firm in your faith, then you will
not stand at all.*

—Isaiah 7:9 HCSB

How do you define success? Do you define it as the accumulation of material possessions or the adulation of your neighbors? If so, you need to reorder your priorities. Genuine success has little to do with fame or fortune; it has everything to do with God's gift of love and His promise of salvation.

If you have accepted Christ as your personal Savior, you are already a towering success in the eyes of God, but there is still more that you can do. Your task—as a believer who has been touched by the Creator's grace—is to accept the spiritual abundance and peace that He offers through the person of His Son. Then, you can share the healing message of God's love and His abundance with a world that desperately needs both. When you do, you will have reached the pinnacle of success.

Winners see an answer for every problem; losers see a problem in every answer.

Barbara Johnson

Success isn't the key. Faithfulness is.

Joni Eareckson Tada

Nothing I can do will make me special. No awards I can earn will make me a better person. The taproot of my being grows in the rich soil of the being of Christ instead of in the shifting sands of worldly accomplishment.

Leslie Williams

A PRAYER FOR GRACE

Dear Lord, let Your priorities be my priorities. Let Your will be my will. Let Your Word be my guide, and keep me mindful that genuine success is a result, not of the world's approval, but of Your approval. Amen

LIVING COURAGEOUSLY

Be strong and courageous, and do the work. Don't be afraid or discouraged, for the Lord God, my God, is with you. He won't leave you or forsake you.

—1 Chronicles 28:20 HCSB

Christian women have every reason to live courageously. After all, the final battle has already been won on the cross at Calvary. But even dedicated followers of Christ may find their courage tested by the inevitable disappointments and fears that visit the lives of believers and non-believers alike.

When you find yourself worried about the challenges of today or the uncertainties of tomorrow, you must ask yourself whether or not you are ready to place your concerns and your life in God's all-powerful, all-knowing, all-loving hands. If the answer to that question is yes—as it should be—then you can draw courage today from the source of strength that never fails: your Heavenly Father.

What is courage? It is the ability to be strong in trust, in conviction, in obedience. To be courageous is to step out in faith—to trust and obey, no matter what.

Kay Arthur

Just as courage is faith in good, so discouragement is faith in evil, and, while courage opens the door to good, discouragement opens it to evil.

Hannah Whitall Smith

With each new experience of letting God be in control, we gain courage and reinforcement for daring to do it again and again.

Gloria Gaither

A Prayer for Grace

Lord, sometimes, this world can be a fearful place, but You have promised me that You are with me always. Today, Lord, I will live courageously as I place my trust in Your everlasting power and my faith in Your everlasting love. Amen

MAKING THE RIGHT DECISIONS

Now if any of you lacks wisdom, he should ask God, who gives to all generously and without criticizing, and it will be given to him.

—James 1:5 HCSB

Some decisions are easy to make because the consequences of those decisions are small. When the person behind the counter asks, "Want fries with that?" the necessary response requires little thought because the aftermath of that decision is relatively unimportant.

Some decisions, on the other hand, are big . . . very big. If you're facing one of those big decisions, here are some things you can do: 1. Gather as much information as you can: don't expect to get all the facts—that's impossible—but get as many facts as you can in a reasonable amount of time. (Proverbs 24:3-4) 2. Don't be too impulsive: If you have time to make a decision, use that time to make a good decision. (Proverbs 19:2) 3. Rely on the advice of trusted friends and mentors. Proverbs 1:5 makes it clear: "A wise man will hear and increase learning, and a man of understanding will attain wise counsel" (NKJV). 4. Pray for guidance. When you seek it, He will give it. (Luke 11:9) 5. Trust the quiet inner voice of your conscience: Treat your conscience as you would a trusted advisor. (Luke 17:21) 6. When the time for action arrives, act. Procrastination is the enemy of progress; don't let it defeat you. (James 1:22).

People who can never quite seem to make up their minds usually make themselves miserable. So when in doubt, be decisive. It's the decent way to live.

The location of your affections will drive the direction of your decisions.

Lisa Bevere

A PRAYER FOR GRACE

Dear Lord, today I will focus my thoughts on Your will for my life. I will strive to make decisions that are pleasing to You, and I will strive to follow in the footsteps of Your Son. Amen

PRAISING GOD FOR HIS ABUNDANCE

I have come that they may have life, and that they may have it more abundantly.

—John 10:10 NKJV

God's gifts are available to all, but they are not guaranteed; those gifts must be claimed by those who choose to follow Christ. As believers, we are free to accept God's gifts, or not; that choice, and the consequences that result from it, are ours and ours alone.

The 10th chapter of John tells us that Christ came to earth so that our lives might be filled with abundance. But what, exactly, did Jesus mean when He promised "life . . . more abundantly"? Was Jesus referring to material possessions or financial wealth? Hardly. When Jesus declared Himself the shepherd of mankind (John 10:7-9), He offered a different kind of abundance: a spiritual richness that extends beyond the temporal boundaries of this world.

If you are a thoughtful believer, you will open yourself to Christ's spiritual abundance by following Him completely and without reservation. When you do, you will receive the love, the peace, and the joy that He has promised.

Do you sincerely seek the riches that our Savior offers to those who give themselves to Him? Then follow Him—and receive the blessings that He has promised. When you establish an intimate, passionate relationship with Christ, you are then free to claim the love, the protection, and the spiritual abundance that the Shepherd offers His sheep.

A PRAYER FOR GRACE

I praise You, Lord, for the abundant life given through Your Son Jesus Christ. You have blessed me beyond measure. Make me a faithful steward of the gifts You have given me so that I may share Your abundance with all who cross my path. Amen

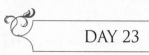

THE NEED FOR SILENCE

Be silent before the Lord and wait expectantly for Him.

—Psalm 37:7 HCSB

The world seems to grow louder day by day, and our senses seem to be invaded at every turn. If we allow the distractions of a clamorous society to separate us from God's peace, we do ourselves a profound disservice. Our task, as dutiful believers, is to carve out moments of silence in a world filled with noise.

If we are to maintain righteous minds and compassionate hearts, we must take time each day for prayer and for meditation. We must make ourselves still in the presence of our Creator. We must quiet our minds and our hearts so that we might sense God's will and His love.

Has the hectic pace of life robbed you of God's peace? If so, it's time to reorder your priorities and your life. Nothing is more important than the time you spend with your Heavenly Father. So be still and claim the genuine peace that is found in the silent moments you spend with God.

If you, too, will learn to wait upon God, to get alone with Him, and remain silent so that you can hear His voice when He is ready to speak to you, what a difference it will make in your life!

Kay Arthur

Because Jesus Christ is our Great High Priest, not only can we approach God without a human "go-between," we can also hear and learn from God in some sacred moments without one.

Beth Moore

A PRAYER FOR GRACE

Dear Lord, in the quiet moments of this day, I will turn my thoughts and prayers to You. In silence I will sense Your presence, and I will seek Your will for my life, knowing that when I accept Your peace, I will be blessed today and throughout eternity. Amen

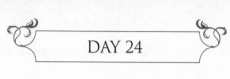

BEING CAREFUL WITH YOUR WORDS

Careful words make for a careful life; careless talk may ruin everything.

—Proverbs 13:3 MSG

How important are the words we speak? More important than we may realize. Our words have echoes that extend beyond place or time. If our words are encouraging, we can lift others up; if our words are hurtful, we can hold others back.

Jesus said, "In everything, do to others what you would have them do to you, for this sums up the Law and the Prophets" (Matthew 7:12 NIV). This commandment is, indeed, the Golden Rule for Christians of every generation. And if we are to observe the Golden Rule, we must be careful to speak words of encouragement, hope, and truth to all those who cross our paths.

Do you seek to be a source of encouragement to others? And, do you seek to be a worthy ambassador for Christ? If so, you must speak words that are worthy of your Savior. So avoid angry outbursts. Refrain from impulsive outpourings. Terminate tantrums. Instead, speak words of encouragement and hope to your family and friends, who, by the way, need all the hope and encouragement they can find.

The things that we feel most deeply we ought to learn to be silent about, at least until we have talked them over thoroughly with God.

Elisabeth Elliot

A PRAYER FOR GRACE

Lord, You have warned me that I will be judged by the words I speak. And, You have commanded me to choose my words carefully so that I might be a source of encouragement and hope to all whom I meet. Keep me mindful, Lord, that I have influence on many people . . . make me an influence for good. And may the words that I speak today be worthy of the One who has saved me forever. Amen

PRAISE HIM

Praise the Lord, all nations! Glorify Him, all peoples! For great is His faithful love to us; the Lord's faithfulness endures forever. Hallelujah!

—Psalm 117 HCSB

Because we have been saved by God's only Son, we must never lose hope in the priceless gifts of eternal love and eternal life. And, because we are so richly blessed, we must approach our Heavenly Father with reverence and thanksgiving.

Sometimes, in our rush "to get things done," we simply don't stop long enough to pause and thank our Creator for the countless blessings He has bestowed upon us. But when we slow down and express our gratitude to the One who made us, we enrich our own lives and the lives of those around us.

Thanksgiving should become a habit, a regular part of our daily routines. God has blessed us beyond measure, and we owe Him everything,

including our eternal praise. Let us praise Him today, tomorrow, and throughout eternity.

Our God is the sovereign Creator of the universe! He loves us as His own children and has provided every good thing we have; He is worthy of our praise every moment.

Shirley Dobson

Two wings are necessary to lift our souls toward God: prayer and praise. Prayer asks. Praise accepts the answer.

Mrs. Charles E. Cowman

A PRAYER FOR GRACE

Dear Lord, today and every day I will praise You. I come to You with hope in my heart and words of thanksgiving on my lips. Let me follow in Christ's footsteps, and let my thoughts, my prayers, my words, and my deeds honor You now and forever. Amen

GOD'S CALLING

I, therefore, the prisoner in the Lord, urge you to walk worthy of the calling you have received.

—Ephesians 4:1 HCSB

It is terribly important that you heed God's calling by discovering and developing your talents and your spiritual gifts. If you seek to make a difference—and if you seek to bear eternal fruit—you must discover your gifts and begin using them for the glory of God.

Every believer has at least one gift. In John 15:16, Jesus says, "You did not choose Me, but I chose you and appointed you that you should go and bear fruit, and that your fruit should remain, that whatever you ask the Father in My name He may give you." Have you found your special calling? If not, keep searching and keep praying until you find it. God has important work for you to do, and the time to begin that work is now.

If God's Word, your circumstances, and the counsel of others line up, and if you sense his provision, I'd say go for it.

Luci Swindoll

From the very moment one feels called to act is born the strength to bear whatever horror one will feel or see. In some inexplicable way, terror loses its overwhelming power when it becomes a task that must be faced.

Emmi Bonhoeffer

A Prayer for Grace

Heavenly Father, You have called me, and I acknowledge that calling. In these quiet moments before this busy day unfolds, I come to You. I will study Your Word and seek Your guidance. Give me the wisdom to know Your will for my life and the courage to follow wherever You may lead me, today and forever. Amen

MAKING TIME
FOR GOD

Don't burn out; keep yourselves fueled and aflame.
Be alert servants of the Master, cheerfully expectant.
Don't quit in hard times; pray all the harder.

—Romans 12:11-12 MSG

H as the busy pace of life robbed you of
the peace that might otherwise be yours
through Jesus Christ? If so, you are simply too busy for your own good. Through His Son
Jesus, God offers you a peace that passes human
understanding, but He won't force His peace
upon you; in order to experience it, you must
slow down long enough to sense His presence
and His love.

Each waking moment holds the potential
to think a creative thought or offer a heartfelt
prayer. So even if you're a woman with too many
demands and too few hours in which to meet
them, don't panic. Instead, be comforted in
the knowledge that when you sincerely seek to

discover God's purpose for your life, He will respond in marvelous and surprising ways. Remember: this is the day that He has made and that He has filled it with countless opportunities to love, to serve, and to seek His guidance. Seize those opportunities today, and keep seizing them every day that you live.

There is an enormous power in little things to distract our attention from God.

Oswald Chambers

A PRAYER FOR GRACE

Dear Lord, You are my rock, and I praise You for Your blessings. But sometimes, I am distracted by the busyness of the day or the demands of the moment. When I am worried or anxious, Father, turn my thoughts back to You. Help me to trust Your will, to follow Your commands, and to accept Your peace, today and forever. Amen

WHAT'S REALLY IMPORTANT

And He told them, "Watch out and be on guard against all greed, because one's life is not in the abundance of his possessions."

—Luke 12:15 HCSB

D o you sometimes feel swamped by your possessions? Do you seem to be spending more and more time keeping track of the things you own while making mental notes of the things you intend to buy? If so, here's a word of warning: your fondness for material possessions is getting in the way of your relationships—your relationships with the people around you and your relationship with God.

Society teaches us to honor possessions . . . God teaches us to honor people. And if we seek to be worthy followers of Christ, we must never invest too much energy in the acquisition of "stuff." Earthly riches are here today and all too soon gone. Our real riches, of course, are in heaven, and that's where we should focus our thoughts and our energy.

Outside appearances, things like the clothes you wear or the car you drive, are important to other people but totally unimportant to God. Trust God.

Marie T. Freeman

As faithful stewards of what we have, ought we not to give earnest thought to our staggering surplus?

Elisabeth Elliot

A PRAYER FOR GRACE

Dear Lord, keep me mindful that material possessions cannot bring me joy—my joy comes from You. I praise You, Father for Your gifts. Let me feel Your presence and share Your love with family, with friends, and with neighbors, this day and every day. Amen

THE IMPORTANCE OF DISCIPLINE

I discipline my body and bring it under strict control, so that after preaching to others, I myself will not be disqualified.

—1 Corinthians 9:27 HCSB

God's Word is clear: as believers, we are called to lead lives of discipline, diligence, moderation, and maturity. But the world often tempts us to behave otherwise. Everywhere we turn, or so it seems, we are faced with powerful temptations to behave in undisciplined, ungodly ways.

We live in a world in which leisure is glorified and misbehavior is glamorized. But God has other plans. He did not create us for lives of mischief or mediocrity; He created us for far greater things.

Life's greatest rewards seldom fall into our laps; to the contrary, God rewards diligence and righteousness just as certainly as He punishes laziness and sin. As believers in a just God, we should behave accordingly.

The balance of affirmation and discipline, freedom and restraint, encouragement and warning is different for each child and season and generation, yet the absolutes of God's Word are necessary and trustworthy no matter how mercuric the time.

Gloria Gaither

A PRAYER FOR GRACE

Heavenly Father, You are my rock and my protector, and I praise You. Make me a woman who understands the need to live a disciplined life. Let me teach others by the faithfulness of my conduct, and let me follow Your will and Your Word, today and every day. Amen

BEYOND DISCOURAGEMENT

He gives power to the weak, and to those who have no might He increases strength.

—Isaiah 40:29 NKJV

We Christians have many reasons to celebrate. God is in His heaven; Christ has risen, and we are the sheep of His flock. Yet sometimes, even the most devout believers may become discouraged. After all, we live in a world where expectations can be high and demands can be even higher.

When we fail to meet the expectations of others (or, for that matter, the expectations that we have for ourselves), we may be tempted to abandon hope. But God has other plans. He knows exactly how He intends to use us. Our task is to remain faithful until He does.

If you're a woman who has become discouraged with the direction of your day or your life, turn your thoughts and prayers to God. He is a

God of possibility, not negativity. He will help you count your blessings instead of your hardships. And then, with a renewed spirit of optimism and hope, you can properly thank your Father in heaven for His blessings, for His love, and for His Son.

Just as courage is faith in good, so discouragement is faith in evil, and, while courage opens the door to good, discouragement opens it to evil.

Hannah Whitall Smith

A PRAYER FOR GRACE

Dear Lord, when I am discouraged, give me perspective and faith. When I am weak, give me strength. When I am fearful, give me courage for the day ahead. I will trust in Your promises, Father, and I will live with the assurance that You are with me not only for this day, but also throughout all eternity. Amen

BEYOND DOUBT

*Immediately the father of the child cried out and said
with tears, "Lord, I believe; help my unbelief!"*
—Mark 9:24 NKJV

I f you've never had any doubts about your
faith, then you can stop reading this page
now and skip to the next chapter. But if
you've ever been plagued by doubts about your
faith or your God, keep reading.

Even some of the most faithful Christians
are, at times, beset by occasional bouts of discouragement and doubt. But even when we feel
far removed from God, God is never far removed
from us. He is always with us, always willing to
calm the storms of life—always willing to replace
our doubts with comfort and assurance.

Whenever you're plagued by doubts, that's
precisely the moment you should seek God's presence by genuinely seeking to establish a deeper,
more meaningful relationship with His Son.
Then you may rest assured that in time, God will

calm your fears, answer your prayers, and restore your confidence.

Fear and doubt are conquered by a faith that rejoices. And faith can rejoice because the promises of God are as certain as God Himself.

Kay Arthur

A life lived in God is not lived on the plane of feelings, but of the will.

Elisabeth Elliot

A PRAYER FOR GRACE

Dear God, sometimes this world can be a puzzling place, filled with uncertainty and doubt. When I am unsure of my next step, keep me mindful that You are always near and that You can overcome any challenge. Give me faith, Father, and let me remember always that with Your love and Your power, I can live courageously and faithfully today and every day. Amen

A SPIRITUAL SICKNESS

All bitterness, anger and wrath, insult and slander must be removed from you, along with all wickedness. And be kind and compassionate to one another, forgiving one another, just as God also forgave you in Christ.

—Ephesians 4:31-32 HCSB

Are you a woman who is mired in the quicksand of bitterness or regret? If so, you are not only disobeying God's Word, you are also wasting your time. The world holds few if any rewards for those who remain angrily focused upon the past. Still, the act of forgiveness is difficult for all but the most saintly men and women.

Being frail, fallible, imperfect human beings, most of us are quick to anger, quick to blame, slow to forgive, and even slower to forget. Yet as Christians, we are commanded to forgive others, just as we, too, have been forgiven.

If there exists even one person—alive or dead—against whom you hold bitter feelings, it's time to forgive. Or, if you are embittered against yourself for some past mistake or shortcoming, it's finally time to forgive yourself and move on. Hatred, bitterness, and regret are not part of God's plan for your life. Forgiveness is.

Forgiveness is the key which unlocks the door of resentment and the handcuffs of hatred. It breaks the chains of bitterness and the shackles of selfishness.

Corrie ten Boom

A PRAYER FOR GRACE

Dear Lord, free me from the poison of bitterness and the futility of blame. When I am bitter, I cannot sense Your presence; when I blame others, I cannot sense Your peace. Let me turn away from destructive emotions so that I may know the perfect peace and spiritual abundance that can be mine through Your Son, and when I discover His peace, let me share it with praise on my lips and love in my heart. Amen

PRAISING GOD FOR HIS WORD

Man shall not live by bread alone, but by every word that proceeds from the mouth of God.

—Matthew 4:4 NKJV

God's Word is unlike any other book. The Bible is a roadmap for life here on earth and for life eternal. As Christians, we are called upon to study God's Holy Word, to trust His Word, to follow its commandments, and to share its Good News with the world.

The words of Matthew 4:4 remind us that, "Man shall not live by bread alone but by every word that proceedeth out of the mouth of God" (KJV). As believers, we must study the Bible and meditate upon its meaning for our lives. Otherwise, we deprive ourselves of a priceless gift from our Creator.

Warren Wiersbe observed, "When the child of God looks into the Word of God, he sees the Son of God. And, he is transformed by the Spirit of God to share in the glory of God." God's Holy Word is, indeed, a transforming, life-changing, one-of-a-kind treasure. And, a passing acquaintance with the Good Book is insufficient for Christians who seek to obey God's Word and to understand His will. After all, man does not live by bread alone . . .

Study the Bible and observe how the persons behaved and how God dealt with them. There is explicit teaching on every condition of life.

Corrie ten Boom

A Prayer for Grace

Dear Lord, the Bible is Your gift to me; thank You. When I stray from Your Holy Word, Father, I suffer. But, when I place Your Word at the very center of my life, I am protected and blessed. Make me a faithful student of Your Word today and every day. Amen

GOD'S LOVE

The Lord is gracious and compassionate, slow to anger and great in faithful love. The Lord is good to everyone; His compassion [rests] on all He has made.

—Psalm 145:8-9 HCSB

God's love for you is deeper and more profound than you can fathom. And now, precisely because you are a wondrous creation treasured by God, a question presents itself: What will you do in response to God's love? Will you ignore it or embrace it? Will you return it or neglect it? The decision, of course, is yours and yours alone.

When you embrace God's love, you are forever changed. When you embrace God's love, you feel differently about yourself, your neighbors, and your world. When you embrace God's love, you share His message and you obey His commandments.

When you accept the Heavenly Father's grace and share His love, you are blessed here on earth and throughout all eternity. Accept His love today.

No matter what we've been, when we are touched by God, we can honestly say, "Now I'm no longer the same!"

Gloria Gaither

God loves us enough to make us ultimately miserable in our rebellion.

Beth Moore

A PRAYER FOR GRACE

Thank You, Lord, for Your love. Your love is boundless, infinite, and eternal. Today, let me pause and reflect upon Your love for me, and let me share that love with all those who cross my path. Amen

TRUSTING GOD'S WISDOM

Happy is the person who finds wisdom and gains understanding.

—Proverbs 3:13 NLT

Sometimes, amid the concerns of everyday life, we lose perspective. Life seems out of balance as we confront an array of demands that sap our strength and cloud our thoughts. What's needed is a renewed faith, a fresh perspective, and God's wisdom.

Here in the 21st century, commentary is commonplace and information is everywhere. But the ultimate source of wisdom, the kind of timeless wisdom that God willingly shares with His children, is still available from a single unique source: the Holy Bible.

The wisdom of the world changes with the ever-shifting sands of public opinion. God's wisdom does not. His wisdom is eternal. It never changes. And it most certainly is the wisdom that you must use to plan your day, your life, and your eternal destiny.

This is my song through endless ages: Jesus led me all the way.

Fanny Crosby

Wisdom is knowledge applied. Head knowledge is useless on the battlefield. Knowledge stamped on the heart makes one wise.

Beth Moore

A PRAYER FOR GRACE

Dear Lord, when I trust in the wisdom of the world, I am often led astray, but when I trust in Your wisdom, I build my life upon a firm foundation. Today and every day I will trust Your Word and follow it, knowing that the ultimate wisdom is Your wisdom and the ultimate truth is Your truth. Amen

TRUST HIS PERFECT PLAN

You will show me the path of life; in Your presence is fullness of joy; at Your right hand are pleasures forevermore.

—Psalm 16:11 NKJV

God has a plan for your life. He understands that plan as thoroughly and completely as He knows you. And, if you seek God's will earnestly and prayerfully, He will make His plans known to you in His own time and in His own way.

If you sincerely seek to live in accordance with God's will for your life, you will live in accordance with His commandments. You will study God's Word, and you will be watchful for His signs.

Sometimes, God's plans seem unmistakably clear to you. But other times, He may lead you through the wilderness before He directs you to the Promised Land. So be patient and keep seeking His will for your life. When you do, you'll be amazed at the marvelous things that an all-powerful, all-knowing God can do.

I'm convinced that there is nothing that can happen to me in this life that is not precisely designed by a sovereign Lord to give me the opportunity to learn to know Him.

Elisabeth Elliot

A PRAYER FOR GRACE

Lord, You have a plan for my life that is grander than I can imagine. Let Your purposes be my purposes. Let Your will be my will. When I am confused, give me clarity. When I am frightened, give me courage. Let me be Your faithful servant, always seeking Your guidance for my life. And, let me always be a shining beacon for Your Son today and every day that I live. Amen

INTEGRITY ALWAYS

The godly walk with integrity; blessed are their children after them.

—Proverbs 20:7 NLT

Wise women understand that integrity is a crucial building block in the foundation of a well-lived life. Integrity is built slowly over a lifetime. It is the sum of every right decision, every honest word, every noble thought, and every heartfelt prayer. It is forged on the anvil of honorable work and polished by the twin virtues of generosity and humility. Integrity is a precious thing—difficult to build, but easy to tear down.

As believers in Christ, we must seek to live each day with discipline, honesty, and faith. When we do, at least two things happen: integrity becomes a habit, and God blesses us because of our obedience to Him.

Living a life of integrity isn't always the easiest way, but it is always the right way. And God clearly intends that it should be our way, too.

God never called us to naïveté. He called us to integrity . . . . The biblical concept of integrity emphasizes mature innocence not childlike ignorance.

Beth Moore

Integrity is not a given factor in everyone's life. It is a result of self-discipline, inner trust, and a decision to be relentlessly honest in all situations in our lives.

John Maxwell

Often, our character is at greater risk in prosperity than in adversity.

Beth Moore

A PRAYER FOR GRACE

Dear Lord, You search my heart and know me far better than I know myself. May I be Your worthy servant, and may I live according to Your commandments. Let me be a woman of integrity, Lord, and let my words and deeds be a testimony to You, today and always. Amen

LOOKING FOR MIRACLES

Looking at them, Jesus said, "With men it is impossible, but not with God, because all things are possible with God."

—Mark 10:27 HCSB

D o you believe in an all-powerful God who can do miraculous things in you and through you? You should. But perhaps, as you have faced the inevitable struggles of life-here-on-earth, you have—without realizing it—placed limitations on God. To do so is a profound mistake. God's power has no such limitations, and He can work mighty miracles in your own life if you let Him.

Do you lack a firm faith in God's power to perform miracles for you and your loved ones? If so, you are attempting to place limitations on a God who has none. Instead of doubting your Heavenly Father, you must place yourself in His hands. Instead of doubting God's power, you must trust it. Expect Him to work miracles, and be watchful. With God, absolutely nothing is impossible, including an amazing assortment of miracles that He stands ready, willing, and perfectly able to perform for you and yours.

The most profane word we use is "hopeless." When you say a situation or person is hopeless, you are slamming the door in the face of God.

Kathy Troccoli

A PRAYER FOR GRACE

Heavenly Father, Your infinite power is beyond human understanding. With You, Lord, nothing is impossible. Keep me always mindful of Your power, and let me share the glorious message of Your miracles. When I lose hope, give me faith; when others lose hope, let me tell them of Your glory and Your works. Today, Lord, let me expect the miraculous, let me praise You, and let me give thanks for Your miracles. Amen

KINDNESS NOW

If you really carry out the royal law prescribed in Scripture, You shall love your neighbor as yourself, you are doing well.

—James 2:8 HCSB

In the busyness and confusion of daily life, it is easy to lose focus, and it is easy to become frustrated. We are imperfect human beings struggling to manage our lives as best we can, but we often fall short. When we are distracted or disappointed, we may neglect to share a kind word or a kind deed. This oversight hurts others, but it hurts us most of all.

Kindness is a choice. Sometimes, when we feel happy or prosperous, we find it easy to be kind. Other times, when we are discouraged or tired, we can scarcely summon the energy to utter a single kind word. But, God's commandment is clear: we must observe the Golden Rule "in everything." God intends that we make the conscious choice to treat others with kindness and respect, no matter our circumstances, no matter our emotions. Kindness, therefore, is a choice that we, as Christians must make many times each day.

When we weave the thread of kindness into the very fabric of our lives, we give a priceless gift to others, and we give glory to the One who gave His life for us. As believers, we must do no less.

Sometimes one little spark of kindness is all it takes to reignite the light of hope in a heart that's blinded by pain.

Barbara Johnson

A PRAYER FOR GRACE

Help me, Lord, to see the needs of those around me. Today, let me show courtesy to those who cross my path. Today, let me spread kind words in honor of Your Son. Today, let forgiveness rule my heart. And every day, Lord, let my love for Christ be demonstrated through the acts of kindness that I offer to those who need the healing touch of the Master's hand. Amen

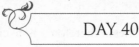

FINDING COMFORT

This is my comfort in my affliction: Your promise has given me life.

—Psalm 119:50 HCSB

As Christians, we can be assured of this fact: Whether we find ourselves on the pinnacle of the mountain or in the darkest depths of the valley, God is there.

If you have been touched by the transforming love of Jesus, then you have every reason to live courageously. After all, Christ has already won the ultimate battle—and He won it for you—on the cross at Calvary. Still, even if you are a dedicated Christian, you may find yourself discouraged by the inevitable disappointments and tragedies that occur in the lives of believers and non-believers alike.

The next time you find your courage tested to the limit, lean upon God's promises. Trust His Son. Remember that God is always near and that He is your protector and your deliverer. When you are worried, anxious, or afraid, call upon Him and accept the touch of His comforting hand. Remember that God rules both mountaintops and valleys—with limitless wisdom and love— now and forever.

O Lord, thank You that Your side of the embroidery of our life is always perfect. That is such a comfort when our side is sometimes so mixed up.

Corrie ten Boom

Put your hand into the hand of God. He gives the calmness and serenity of heart and soul.

Mrs. Charles E. Cowman

A PRAYER FOR GRACE

Today, Lord, let me count my blessings with thanksgiving in my heart. You have cared for me, Lord, and I will give You the glory and the praise. Let me accept Your blessings and Your gifts, and let me share them with others, just as You first shared them with me. Amen

THE GIFT OF LIFE

Seek the Lord, and ye shall live....

—Amos 5:6 KJV

Life is a glorious gift from God. Treat it that way—and while you're at it, praise the Giver for His gift.

This day, like every other, is filled to the brim with opportunities, challenges, and choices. But, no choice that you make is more important than the choice you make concerning God. Today, you will either place Him at the center of your life—or not—and the consequences of that choice have implications that are both temporal and eternal.

Sometimes, without our even realizing it, we gradually drift away from the One we need most. Thankfully, God never drifts away from us. He remains always present, always steadfast, always loving.

As you begin this day, place God and His Son where they belong: in your head, in your prayers, on your lips, and in your heart. And then, with God as your guide and companion, let the journey begin . . .

We are common earthenware jars, filled with the treasure of the riches of God. The jar is not important—the treasure is everything.

Corrie ten Boom

As I contemplate all the sacrifices required in order to live a life that is totally focused on Jesus Christ and His eternal kingdom, the joy seeps out of my heart onto my face in a smile of deep satisfaction.

Anne Graham Lotz

A PRAYER FOR GRACE

Lord, You are the Giver of all life. Let me live a life that pleases You, and let me thank You always for Your blessings. You love me and protect me, Heavenly Father. Let me be grateful, and let me live for You today and throughout eternity. Amen

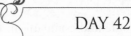

DAY 42

HE IS HERE

I am not alone, because the Father is with Me.

—John 16:32 HCSB

Since God is everywhere, we are free to sense His presence whenever we take the time to quiet our souls and turn our prayers to Him. But sometimes, amid the incessant demands of everyday life, we turn our thoughts far from God; when we do, we suffer.

Do you set aside quiet moments each day to offer praise to your Creator? As a woman who has received the gift of God's grace, you most certainly should. Silence is a gift that you give to yourself and to God. During these moments of stillness, you will often sense the infinite love and power of your Creator—and He, in turn, will speak directly to your heart.

The familiar words of Psalm 46:10 remind us to "Be still, and know that I am God." When we do so, we encounter the awesome presence of our loving Father, and we are comforted in the knowledge that God is not just near. He is here.

It's a crazy world and life speeds by at a blur, yet God is right in the middle of the craziness. And anywhere, at anytime, we may turn to Him, hear His voice, feel His hand, and catch the fragrance of heaven.

Joni Eareckson Tada

We will not fully realize the cost of sin until we finally sit at His feet and know the inexpressible joy of His presence. How can we know what we have lost until we have regained it?

Beth Moore

A PRAYER FOR GRACE

Dear Lord, You are with me always, and I praise You for Your love. Help me feel Your presence in every situation and every circumstance. Today, Father, I will acknowledge Your presence, Your love, and Your Son. Amen

DAY 43

ACCEPTANCE TODAY

One thing I do, forgetting those things which are behind and reaching forward to those things which are ahead, I press toward the goal for the prize of the upward call of God in Christ Jesus.

—Philippians 3:13-14 NKJV

Manmade plans are fallible; God's plans are not. Yet whenever life takes an unexpected turn, we are tempted to fall into the spiritual traps of worry, self-pity, or bitterness. God intends that we do otherwise.

The old saying is familiar: "Forgive and forget." But when we have been hurt badly, forgiveness is often difficult and forgetting is downright impossible. Since we can't forget yesterday's troubles, we should learn from them. Yesterday has much to teach us about tomorrow. We may learn from the past, but we should never live in the past.

So if you're trying to forget the past, don't waste your time. Instead, try a different approach: learn to accept the past and live in the present. Then, you can focus your thoughts and your energies, not on the struggles of yesterday, but instead on the profound opportunities that God has placed before you today.

Surrender to the Lord is not a tremendous sacrifice, not an agonizing performance. It is the most sensible thing you can do.

Corrie ten Boom

A Prayer for Grace

Lord, when I am discouraged, give me hope. When I am impatient, give me peace. When I face circumstances that I cannot change, give me a spirit of acceptance. In all things great and small, let me trust in You, Dear Lord, knowing that You are the Giver of life and the Giver of all things good, today and forever. Amen

THE RIGHT PRIORITIES

First pay attention to me, and then relax. Now you can take it easy—you're in good hands.

—Proverbs 1:33 MSG

"First things first." These words are easy to speak but hard to put into practice. For busy women living in a demanding world, placing first things first can be difficult indeed. Why? Because so many people are expecting so many things from us!

If you're having trouble prioritizing your day, perhaps you've been trying to organize your life according to your own plans, not God's. A better strategy, of course, is to take your daily obligations and place them in the hands of the One who created you. To do so, you must prioritize your day according to God's commandments, and you must seek His will and His wisdom in all matters. Then, you can face the day with the assurance that the same God who created our universe out of nothingness will help you place first things first in your own life.

Do you feel overwhelmed or confused? Turn the concerns of this day over to God—prayerfully, earnestly, and often. Then listen for His answer . . . and trust the answer He gives.

Great relief and satisfaction can come from seeking God's priorities for us in each season, discerning what is "best" in the midst of many noble opportunities, and pouring our most excellent energies into those things.

Beth Moore

A PRAYER FOR GRACE

Dear Lord, let Your priorities be my priorities. Let Your will be my will. Let Your Word be my guide, and let me grow in faith and in wisdom this day and every day. Amen

MANAGING CHANGE

One Lord, one faith, one baptism, one God and Father of all, who is above all and through all and in all.

—Ephesians 4:5-6 HCSB

Our world is in a state of constant change. God is not. At times, the world seems to be trembling beneath our feet. But we can be comforted in the knowledge that our Heavenly Father is the rock that cannot be shaken. His Word promises, "I am the Lord, I do not change" (Malachi 3:6 NKJV).

Every day that we live, we mortals encounter a multitude of changes—some good, some not so good. And on occasion, all of us must endure life-changing personal losses that leave us breathless. When we do, our loving Heavenly Father stands ready to protect us, to comfort us, to guide us, and, in time, to heal us.

Are you facing difficult circumstances or unwelcome changes? If so, please remember that God is far bigger than any problem you may face. So, instead of worrying about life's inevitable challenges, put your faith in the Father and His only begotten Son: "Jesus Christ is the same yesterday, today, and forever" (Hebrews 13:8 HCSB). And rest assured: It is precisely because your Savior does not change that you can face your challenges with courage for this day and hope for the future.

Conditions are always changing; therefore, I must not be dependent upon conditions. What matters supremely is my soul and my relationship to God.

Corrie ten Boom

A PRAYER FOR GRACE

Dear Lord, our world is constantly changing. When I face the inevitable transitions of life, I will turn to You for strength and assurance. Thank You, Father, for love that is unchanging and everlasting. Amen

HE REWARDS INTEGRITY

In all things showing yourself to be a pattern of good works; in doctrine showing integrity, reverence, incorruptibility . . . .

—Titus 2:7 NKJV

Beth Moore correctly observed, "Those who walk in truth walk in liberty." Godly men and women agree. As believers in Christ, we must seek to live each day with discipline, honesty, and faith. When we do, at least two things happen: integrity becomes a habit, and God blesses us because of our obedience to Him. Living a life of integrity isn't always the easiest way, but it is always the right way . . . and God clearly intends that it should be our way, too.

Character isn't built overnight; it is built slowly over a lifetime. It is the sum of every sensible choice, every honorable decision, and every honest word. It is forged on the anvil of sincerity and polished by the virtue of fairness. Character is a precious thing—preserve yours at all costs.

So, the next time you're tempted to bend the truth—or to break it—ask yourself this simple question: "What does God want me to do?" Then listen carefully to your conscience. When you do, your actions will be honorable, and your character will take care of itself.

There is something about having endured great loss that brings purity of purpose and strength of character.

Barbara Johnson

A PRAYER FOR GRACE

Dear Lord, every day can be an exercise in character-building, and that's what I intend to make this day. I will be mindful that my thoughts and actions have great consequences in my own life and in the lives of my loved ones. I will strive to make my thoughts and actions pleasing to You, so that I may be an instrument of Your peace, today and every day. Amen

BEYOND TEMPTATION

Then Jesus told him, "Go away, Satan! For it is written: You must worship the Lord your God, and you must serve Him only."

—Matthew 4:10 HCSB

After fasting forty days and nights in the desert, Jesus was tempted by Satan. Christ used scripture to rebuke the devil (Matthew 4:1-11). We must do likewise. The Holy Bible provides us with a perfect blueprint for righteous living. If we consult that blueprint daily and follow it carefully, we build our lives according to God's plan.

We live in a world that is brimming with opportunities to stray from God's will. Ours is a society filled with temptations, a place where it is all too easy to disobey God. We, like our Savior, must guard ourselves against these temptations. We do so, in part, through prayer and through a careful reading of God's Word.

The battle against Satan is ongoing. Be vigilant, and call upon your Heavenly Father to protect you. When you petition Him with a sincere heart, God will be your shield, now and forever.

Temptation is not a sin. Even Jesus was tempted. The Lord Jesus gives you the strength needed to resist temptation.

Corrie ten Boom

A PRAYER FOR GRACE

Dear Lord, this world is filled with temptations, distractions, and frustrations. When I turn my thoughts away from You and Your Word, Lord, I suffer bitter consequences. But, when I trust in Your commandments, I am safe. Direct my path far from the temptations and distractions of the world. Let me discover Your will and follow it, Dear Lord, this day and always. Amen

BEYOND
THE FRUSTRATIONS

Don't let your spirit rush to be angry, for anger abides in the heart of fools.

—Ecclesiastes 7:9 HCSB

Sometimes, anger is appropriate. Even Jesus became angry when confronted with the moneychangers in the temple. On occasion, you, like Jesus, will confront evil, and when you do, you may respond as He did: vigorously and without reservation. But, more often than not, your frustrations will be of the more mundane variety. As long as you live here on earth, you will face countless opportunities to lose your temper over small, relatively insignificant events: a traffic jam, a spilled cup of coffee, an inconsiderate comment, or a broken promise. When you are tempted to lose your temper over the minor inconveniences of life, don't. Turn away from anger, hatred, bitterness, and regret. Turn instead to God.

Life is too short to spend it being angry, bored, or dull.

Barbara Johnson

When something robs you of your peace of mind, ask yourself if it is worth the energy you are expending on it. If not, then put it out of your mind in an act of discipline. Every time the thought of "it" returns, refuse it.

Kay Arthur

A PRAYER FOR GRACE

Lord, sometimes, I am quick to anger and slow to forgive. But I know, Lord, that You seek abundance and peace for my life. Forgiveness is Your commandment; empower me to follow the example of Your Son Jesus who forgave His persecutors. Today, as I turn away from anger, I will claim the peace that You intend for my life, and I will praise You for Your blessings. Amen

LAUGH!

A cheerful disposition is good for your health; gloom and doom leave you bone-tired.

—Proverbs 17:22 MSG

L aughter is medicine for the soul, but sometimes, amid the stresses of the day, we forget to take our medicine. Instead of viewing our world with a mixture of optimism and humor, we allow worries and distractions to rob us of the joy that God intends for our lives.

So the next time you find yourself dwelling upon the negatives of life, refocus your attention to things positive. And, if you see your glass as "half empty," rest assured that your spiritual vision is impaired. With God, your glass is never half empty. With God as your protector and Christ as your Savior, your glass is filled to the brim and overflowing…forever.

Today, as you go about your daily activities, approach life with a smile on your lips and hope in your heart. And laugh every chance you get.

Laughter dulls the sharpest pain and flattens out the greatest stress. To share it is to give a gift of health.

Barbara Johnson

We may run, walk, stumble, drive, or fly, but let us never lose sight of the reason for the journey, or miss a chance to see a rainbow on the way.

Gloria Gaither

When you have good, healthy relationships with your family and friends you're more prompted to laugh and not to take yourself so seriously.

Dennis Swanberg

A PRAYER FOR GRACE

Dear Lord, You have given me so many reasons to celebrate life. Today, let me be a joyful Christian—quick to smile and quick to laugh. And, let Your love shine in me and through me, this day and forever. Amen

PRAISING GOD FOR HIS GIFTS

The Lord reigns; let the earth rejoice.

—Psalm 97:1 NKJV

The Lord intends that believers should share His love with His joy in their hearts. Yet sometimes, amid the inevitable hustle and bustle of life-here-on-earth, we can forfeit—albeit temporarily—God's joy as we wrestle with the challenges of daily living.

Joni Eareckson Tada spoke for Christian women of every generation when she observed, "I wanted the deepest part of me to vibrate with that ancient yet familiar longing, that desire for something that would fill and overflow my soul."

If, today, your heart is heavy, open the door of your soul to Christ. He will give you peace and joy. And if you already have the joy of Christ in your heart, share it freely, just as Christ freely shared His joy with you.

The Christian lifestyle is not one of legalistic do's and don'ts, but one that is positive, attractive, and joyful.

Vonette Bright

Among the most joyful people I have known have been some who seem to have had no human reason for joy. The sweet fragrance of Christ has shown through their lives.

Elisabeth Elliot

A PRAYER FOR GRACE

Dear Lord, You have given me so many blessings; I will celebrate Your gifts. Make me thankful, loving, responsible, and wise. I praise You, Father, for the gift of Your Son and for the priceless gift of salvation. Make me be a joyful Christian, a worthy example to others, and a dutiful servant to You this day and forever. Amen

ON BEING A HAPPY CHRISTIAN

Happy are those who fear the Lord. Yes, happy are those who delight in doing what he commands.

—Psalm 112:1 NLT

Do you seek happiness, abundance, and contentment? If so, here are some things you should do: Love God and His Son; depend upon God for strength; try, to the best of your abilities, to follow God's will; and strive to obey His Holy Word. When you do these things, you'll discover that happiness goes hand-in-hand with righteousness. The happiest people are not those who rebel against God; the happiest people are those who love God and obey His commandments.

What does life have in store for you? A world full of possibilities (of course it's up to you to seize them) and God's promise of abundance (of course it's up to you to accept it). So, as you embark upon the next phase of your journey, remember to celebrate the life that God has given you. Your Creator has blessed you beyond measure. Honor Him with your prayers, your words, your deeds, and your joy.

Those who are God's without reserve are, in every sense, content.

Hannah Whitall Smith

When we do what is right, we have contentment, peace, and happiness.

Beverly LaHaye

A PRAYER FOR GRACE

Dear Lord, You are my strength and my joy. I will rejoice in the day that You have made, and I will give thanks for the countless blessings that You have given me. Let me be a joyful Christian, Father, as I share the Good News of Your Son, and let me praise You for all the marvelous things You have done. Amen

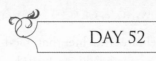

PRAISING GOD FOR HEAVEN

Let not your heart be troubled: ye believe in God, believe also in me. In my Father's house are many mansions: if it were not so, I would have told you. I go to prepare a place for you. And if I go and prepare a place for you, I will come again, and receive you unto myself; that where I am, there ye may be also.

—John 14:1-3 KJV

Sometimes life's inevitable troubles and heartbreaks are easier to tolerate when we remind ourselves that heaven is our true home. An old hymn contains the words, "This world is not my home; I'm just passing through." Thank goodness!

For believers, death is not an ending; it is a beginning. The grave is not a final resting-place; it is a place of transition. Death can never claim those who have accepted Christ as their personal Savior. Christ has promised that He has gone to prepare a glorious home in heaven—a timeless, blessed gift to His children—and Jesus always keeps His promises.

If you've committed your life to Christ, your time here on earth is merely a preparation for a far different life to come: your eternal life with Jesus and a host of fellow believers.

So, while this world can be a place of temporary hardship and temporary suffering, you can be comforted in the knowledge that God offers you a permanent home that is free from all suffering and pain. Please take God at His word. When you do, you can withstand any problem, knowing that your troubles are temporary, but that heaven is not.

A PRAYER FOR GRACE

Dear Lord, I praise You for the gift of eternal life that is mine through Your Son Jesus. I will keep the promise of heaven in my heart today and every day. Amen

LISTENING TO GOD

The one who is from God listens to God's words. This is why you don't listen, because you are not from God.

—John 8:47 HCSB

Sometimes, God displays His wishes in ways that are undeniable. But on other occasions, the hand of God is much more subtle than that. Sometimes, God speaks to us in quiet tones, and when He does, we are well advised to listen . . . carefully.

Do you take time each day for an extended period of silence? And during those precious moments, do you sincerely open your heart to your Creator? If so, you are wise and you are blessed.

The world can be a noisy place, a place filled to the brim with distractions, interruptions, and frustrations. And if you're not careful, the struggles and stresses of everyday living can rob you of the peace that should rightfully be yours because of your personal relationship with Christ. So take time each day to quietly commune with your Savior. When you do, you will most certain-ly encounter the subtle hand of God, and if you are wise, you will let His hand lead you along the path that He has chosen.

We need to stop focusing on our lacks and stop giving out excuses and start looking at and listening to Jesus.

Anne Graham Lotz

In the soul-searching of our lives, we are to stay quiet so we can hear Him say all that He wants to say to us in our hearts.

Charles Swindoll

A PRAYER FOR GRACE

Dear Lord, I have so much to learn and You have so much to teach me. Give me the wisdom to be still and the discernment to hear Your voice, today and every day. Amen

HE GIVES US HOPE

I wait for the Lord; I wait, and put my hope in His word.

—Psalm 130:5 HCSB

Despite God's promises, despite Christ's love, and despite our countless blessings, we frail human beings can still lose hope from time to time. When we do, we need the encouragement of Christian friends, the life-changing power of prayer, and the healing truth of God's Holy Word.

If you find yourself falling into the spiritual traps of worry and discouragement, seek the healing touch of Jesus and the encouraging words of fellow Christians. And remember the words of our Savior: "These things I have spoken unto you, that in me ye might have peace. In the world ye shall have tribulation: but be of good cheer; I have overcome the world" (John 16:33 KJV). This world can be a place of trials and tribulations, but as believers, we are secure. God has promised us peace, joy, and eternal life. And, of course, God keeps His promises today, tomorrow, and forever.

No other religion, no other philosophy promises new bodies, hearts, and minds. Only in the Gospel of Christ do hurting people find such incredible hope.

Joni Eareckson Tada

A PRAYER FOR GRACE

Dear Lord, make me a woman of hope. If I become discouraged, let me turn to You. If I grow weary, let me seek strength in You. When I face disappointments, let me seek Your will and trust Your Word. In every aspect of my life, I will trust You, Father, so that my heart will be filled with faith, hope, and praise, this day and forever. Amen

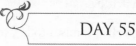

MAKING PEACE WITH THE PAST

Do not remember the past events, pay no attention to things of old. Look, I am about to do something new; even now it is coming. Do you not see it? Indeed, I will make a way in the wilderness, rivers in the desert.

—Isaiah 43:18-19 HCSB

The American theologian Reinhold Niebuhr composed a profoundly simple verse that came to be known as the Serenity Prayer: "God, grant me the serenity to accept the things I cannot change, the courage to change the things I can, and the wisdom to know the difference." Niebuhr's words are far easier to recite than they are to live by. Why? Because most of us want life to unfold in accordance with our own wishes and timetables. But sometimes God has other plans.

One of the things that fits nicely into the category of "things we cannot change" is the past. Yet even though we know that the past is unchangeable, many of us continue to invest energy worrying about the unfairness of yesterday (when we should be focusing on the opportunities of today and the promises of tomorrow).

So, if you've endured a difficult past, accept it and learn from it, but don't spend too much time here in the precious present fretting over memories of the unchangeable past. Instead, trust God's plan and look to the future. After all, the future is where everything that's going to happen to you from this moment on is going to take place.

No matter what, don't ever let yesterday use up too much of today.

Barbara Johnson

A PRAYER FOR GRACE

Heavenly Father, free me from anger, resentment, and envy. When I am bitter, I cannot feel the peace that You intend for my life. Keep me mindful that forgiveness is Your commandment, and help me accept the past, treasure the present, and trust the future . . . to You. Amen

HE IS YOUR ROCK

The Lord is my rock and my fortress and my deliverer;
the God of my strength, in whom I will trust.

—2 Samuel 22:2-3 NKJV

od has promised to protect us, and He intends to keep His promise. In a world filled with dangers and temptations, God is the ultimate armor. In a world filled with misleading messages, God's Word is the ultimate truth. In a world filled with more frustrations than we can count, God's Son offers the ultimate peace.

As a busy woman, you know from firsthand experience that life is not always easy. But as a recipient of God's grace, you also know that you are protected by a loving Heavenly Father.

In times of trouble, God will comfort you; in times of sorrow, He will dry your tears. When you are troubled, or weak, or sorrowful, God is neither distant nor disinterested. To the contrary, God is always present and always vitally engaged in the events of your life. Reach out to Him, and build your future on the rock that cannot be shaken . . . trust in God and rely upon His provisions. He can provide everything you really need . . . and far, far more.

God will never let you sink under your circumstances. He always provide a safety net and His love always encircles.

Barbara Johnson

He goes before us, follows behind us, and hems us safe inside the realm of His protection.

Beth Moore

A PRAYER FOR GRACE

Lord, You are my Shepherd. You care for me; You comfort me; You watch over me; and You have saved me. I will praise You, Father, for Your glorious works, for Your protection, for Your love, and for Your Son. Amen

BEYOND WORRY

Don't worry about anything, but in everything, through prayer and petition with thanksgiving, let your requests be made known to God.

—Philippians 4:6 HCSB

"Worry does not empty tomorrow of its sorrow; it empties today of its strength." So writes Corrie ten Boom, a woman who survived a Nazi concentration camp during World War II. And while our own situations cannot be compared to Corrie's, we still worry about countless matters both great and small. Even though we are Christians who have been given the assurance of salvation—even though we are Christians who have received the promise of God's love and protection—we find ourselves fretting over the countless details of everyday life. Jesus understood our concerns when He spoke the reassuring words found in Matthew 6: "Therefore I tell you, do not worry about your life . . ."

As you consider the promises of Jesus, remember that God still sits in His heaven and you are His beloved child. Then, perhaps, you will worry a little less and trust God a little more, and that's as it should be because God is trustworthy . . . and you are protected.

Worship and worry cannot live in the same heart; they are mutually exclusive.

Ruth Bell Graham

A Prayer for Grace

Lord, You sent Your Son to live as a man on this earth, and You know what it means to be completely human. You understand my worries and my fears, Lord, and You forgive me when I am weak. When my faith begins to wane, help me, Lord, to trust You more. Then, with Your Holy Word on my lips and with the love of Your Son in my heart, let me live courageously, faithfully, prayerfully, and thankfully today and every day. Amen

WORSHIP HIM

For it is written, "You shall worship the Lord your God, and Him only you shall serve."

—Matthew 4:10 NKJV

All of mankind is engaged in the practice of worship. Some choose to worship God and, as a result, reap the joy that He intends for His children. Others distance themselves from God by worshiping such things as earthly possessions or personal gratification . . . and when they do so, they suffer.

Today, as one way of worshipping God, make every aspect of your life a cause for celebration and praise. Praise God for the blessings and opportunities that He has given you, and live according to the beautiful words found in the 5th chapter of 1 Thessalonians: "Rejoice evermore. Pray without ceasing. In every thing give thanks: for this is the will of God in Christ Jesus concerning you" (vv. 16-18 KJV).

God deserves your worship, your prayers, your praise, and your thanks. And you deserve the joy that is yours when you worship Him with your prayers, with your deeds, and with your life.

To worship Him in truth means to worship Him honestly, without hypocrisy, standing open and transparent before Him.

Anne Graham Lotz

It's our privilege to not only raise our hands in worship but also to combine the visible with the invisible in a rising stream of praise and adoration sent directly to our Father.

Shirley Dobson

A PRAYER FOR GRACE

When I worship You, Lord, You direct my path and You cleanse my heart. Let today and every day be a time of worship and praise. Let me worship You in everything that I think and do. Thank You, Lord, for the priceless gift of Your Son Jesus. Let me be worthy of that gift, and let me give You the praise and the glory forever. Amen

DOING IT NOW, NOT LATER

Therefore, get your minds ready for action, being self-disciplined, and set your hope completely on the grace to be brought to you at the revelation of Jesus Christ.

—1 Peter 1:13 HCSB

The old saying is both familiar and true: actions speak louder than words. And as believers, we must beware: our actions should always give credence to the changes that Christ can make in the lives of those who walk with Him.

God calls upon each of us to act in accordance with His will and with respect for His commandments. If we are to be responsible believers, we must realize that it is never enough simply to hear the instructions of God; we must also live by them. And it is never enough to wait idly by while others do God's work here on earth; we, too, must act. Doing God's work is a responsibility that each of us must bear, and when we do, our loving Heavenly Father rewards our efforts with a bountiful harvest.

A bird does not know it can fly before it uses its wings. We learn God's love in our hearts as soon as we act upon it.

Corrie ten Boom

We spend our lives dreaming of the future, not realizing that a little of it slips away every day.

Barbara Johnson

A PRAYER FOR GRACE

Dear Lord, I have heard Your Word, and I have felt Your presence in my heart; let me act accordingly. Let my words and deeds serve as a testimony to the changes You have made in my life. Today, I will praise You, Father, by following in the footsteps of Your Son, and letting others see Him through me. Amen

DAY 60

THE POWER OF PURPOSE

The lines of purpose in your lives never grow slack, tightly tied as they are to your future in heaven, kept taut by hope.

—Colossians 1:5 MSG

"What on earth does God intend for me to do with my life?" It's an easy question to ask but, for many of us, a difficult question to answer. Why? Because God's purposes aren't always clear to us. Sometimes we wander aimlessly in a wilderness of our own making. And sometimes, we struggle mightily against God in an unsuccessful attempt to find success and happiness through our own means, not His.

Sometimes, God's intentions will be clear to you; other times, God's plan will seem uncertain at best. But even on those difficult days when you are unsure which way to turn, you must never lose sight of these overriding facts: God created

you for a reason; He has important work for you
to do; and He's waiting patiently for you to do it.

And the next step is up to you.

How much of our lives are, well, so daily. How
often our hours are filled with the mundane,
seemingly unimportant things that have to be
done, whether at home or work. These very
"daily" tasks could become a celebration of
praise. "It is through consecration," someone has
said, "that drudgery is made divine."

Gigi Graham Tchividjian

A PRAYER FOR GRACE

Dear Lord, You are the Creator of the universe,
and I know that Your plan for my life is grander
than I can imagine. Let Your purposes be my
purposes, and let me trust in the assurance of
Your promises. Amen

TIME FOR RENEWAL

Take My yoke upon you and learn from Me, because I am gentle and humble in heart, and you will find rest for your souls. For My yoke is easy and My burden is light.

—Matthew 11:29-30 HCSB

For busy women living in a fast-paced world, life may seem like a merry-go-round that never stops turning. If that description seems to fit your life, then you may find yourself running short of patience, or strength, or both. If you're feeling tired or discouraged, there is a source from which you can draw the power needed to recharge your spiritual batteries. That source is God.

Are you exhausted or troubled? Turn your heart toward God in prayer. Are you weak or worried? Take the time—or, more accurately, make the time—to delve deeply into God's Holy Word. Are you spiritually depleted? Call upon fellow believers to support you, and call upon Christ to renew your spirit and your life. When you do, you'll discover that the Creator of the universe stands always ready and always able to create a new sense of wonderment and joy in you.

In those desperate times when we feel like we don't have an ounce of strength, He will gently pick up our heads so that our eyes can behold something—something that will keep His hope alive in us.

Kathy Troccoli

A PRAYER FOR GRACE

Lord, You are my rock and my strength. When I grow weary, let me turn my thoughts and my prayers to You. When I am discouraged, restore my faith in You. Let me always trust in Your promises, Lord, and let me draw strength from those promises and from Your unending love. Amen

THE POWER OF OBEDIENCE

Follow the whole instruction the Lord your God has commanded you, so that you may live, prosper, and have a long life in the land you will possess.

—Deuteronomy 5:33 HCSB

How can we demonstrate our love for God? By accepting His Son as our personal Savior and by placing Christ squarely at the center of our lives and our hearts. Jesus said that if we are to love Him, we must obey His commandments (John 14:15). Thus, our obedience to the Master is an expression of our love for Him.

In Ephesians 2:10 we read, "For we are His workmanship, created in Christ Jesus for good works" (NKJV). These words are instructive: We are not saved by good works, but for good works. Good works are not the root, but rather the fruit of our salvation.

Today, let the fruits of your stewardship be a clear demonstration of your love for Christ.

When you do, your good heart will bring forth many good things for yourself and for God. Christ has given you spiritual abundance and eternal life. You, in turn, owe Him good treasure from a single obedient heart . . . yours.

The pathway of obedience can sometimes be difficult, but it always leads to a strengthening of our inner woman.

Vonette Bright

A Prayer for Grace

Dear Lord, when I obey Your commandments, and when I trust the promises of Your Son, I experience love, peace, and abundance. Direct my path far from the temptations and distractions of this world. And, let me discover Your will and follow it, Dear Lord, this day and always. Amen

DAY 63

THE POWER OF OPTIMISM

Make me to hear joy and gladness.

—Psalm 51:8 KJV

Are you an optimistic, hopeful, enthusiastic Christian? You should be. After all, as a believer, you have every reason to be optimistic about life here on earth and life eternal. As C. H. Spurgeon observed, "Our hope in Christ for the future is the mainstream of our joy." But sometimes, you may find yourself pulled down by the inevitable demands and worries of life-here-on-earth. If you find yourself discouraged, exhausted, or both, then it's time to take your concerns to God. When you do, He will lift your spirits and renew your strength.

Today, make this promise to yourself and keep it: vow to be a hope-filled Christian. Think optimistically about your life, your profession, your family, and your future. Trust your hopes, not your fears. Take time to celebrate God's glorious creation. And then, when you've filled your heart with hope and gladness, share your optimism with others. They'll be better for it, and so will you.

We may run, walk, stumble, drive, or fly, but let us never lose sight of the reason for the journey, or miss a chance to see a rainbow on the way.

Gloria Gaither

If you can't tell whether your glass is half-empty or half-full, you don't need another glass; what you need is better eyesight . . . and a more thankful heart.

Marie T. Freeman

A PRAYER FOR GRACE

Thank You, Lord, for Your infinite love. Make me an optimistic Christian, Father, as I place my hope and my trust in You. Amen

WALKING ON HIS PATH

Then He said to them all, "If anyone desires to come after Me, let him deny himself, and take up his cross daily, and follow Me. For whoever desires to save his life will lose it, but whoever loses his life for My sake will save it."

—Luke 9:23-24 NKJV

When Jesus addressed His disciples, He warned that each one must, "take up his cross and follow Me." The disciples must have known exactly what the Master meant. In Jesus' day, prisoners were forced to carry their own crosses to the location where they would be put to death. Thus, Christ's message was clear: in order to follow Him, Christ's disciples must deny themselves and, instead, trust Him completely. Nothing has changed since then.

If we are to be dutiful disciples of the One from Galilee, we must trust Him and we must follow Him. Jesus never comes "next." He is always first. He shows us the path of life.

Do you seek to be a worthy disciple of Jesus? Then pick up His cross today and follow in His footsteps. When you do, you can walk with confidence: He will never lead you astray.

The cross that Jesus commands you and me to carry is the cross of submissive obedience to the will of God, even when His will includes suffering and hardship and things we don't want to do.

Anne Graham Lotz

A PRAYER FOR GRACE

Lord, sometimes life is difficult. But even when I can't see any hope for the future, You are always with me. And, I can live courageously because I know that You are leading me to a place where I can accomplish Your kingdom's work . . . and where You lead, I will follow. Amen

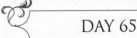

BEYOND PESSIMISM

Why are you cast down, O my soul? And why are you disquieted within me? Hope in God; for I shall yet praise Him, the help of my countenance and my God.

—Psalm 42:11 NKJV

Pessimism and Christianity don't mix. Why? Because Christians have every reason to be optimistic about life here on earth and life eternal.

Sometimes, despite our trust in God, we may fall into the spiritual traps of worry, frustration, anxiety, or sheer exhaustion, and our hearts become heavy. What's needed is plenty of rest, a large dose of perspective, and God's healing touch, but not necessarily in that order.

Today, make this promise to yourself and keep it: vow to be a hope-filled Christian. Think optimistically about your life, your profession, and your future. Trust your hopes, not your fears. Take time to celebrate God's glorious creation. And then, when you've filled your heart with hope and gladness, share your optimism with others. They'll be better for it, and so will you. But not necessarily in that order.

Worry is the darkroom in which negatives are developed.

Anonymous

Never yield to gloomy anticipation. Place your hope and confidence in God. He has no record of failure.

Mrs. Charles E. Cowman

A PRAYER FOR GRACE

Dear Heavenly Father, on those days when I am troubled, You comfort me if I turn my thoughts and prayers to You. When I am afraid, You protect me. When I am discouraged, You lift me up. You are my unending source of strength, Lord. In every circumstance, let me trust Your plan and Your will for my life. Amen

DAY 66

THE POWER OF PATIENCE

A patient person [shows] great understanding, but a quick-tempered one promotes foolishness.

—Proverbs 14:29 HCSB

Are you a woman always in a hurry? If so, you may be in for a few disappointments. Why? Because life has a way of unfolding according to its own timetable, not yours. That's why life requires patience . . . and lots of it!

Most of us are impatient for God to grant us the desires of our heart. Usually, we know what we want, and we know precisely when we want it: right now, if not sooner. But God may have other plans. And when God's plans differ from our own, we must trust in His infinite wisdom and in His infinite love.

Lamentations 3:25 reminds us that, "The Lord is wonderfully good to those who wait for him and seek him" (NIV). But, for most of us, waiting quietly is difficult because we're in such a hurry for things to happen!

The next time you find your patience tested to the limit, slow down, take a deep breath, and relax. Sometimes life can't be hurried—and during those times, patience is indeed a priceless virtue.

How do you wait upon the Lord? First you must learn to sit at His feet and take time to listen to His words.

Kay Arthur

A PRAYER FOR GRACE

Lord, give me patience. When I am hurried, give me peace. When I am frustrated, give me perspective. When I am angry, let me turn my heart to You. Today, let me become a more patient woman, Dear Lord, as I trust in You and in Your master plan for my life. Amen

PRAISING GOD FOR HIS PERFECT TIMING

Therefore humble yourselves under the mighty hand of God, that He may exalt you in due time.

—1 Peter 5:6 NKJV

If you sincerely seek to be a woman of faith, then you must learn to trust God's timing. You will be sorely tempted, however, to do otherwise. Because you are a fallible human being, you are impatient for things to happen. But, God knows better.

God has created a world that unfolds according to His own timetable, not ours . . . thank goodness! We mortals might make a terrible mess of things. God does not.

God's plan does not always happen in the way that we would like or at the time of our own choosing. Our task—as believing Christians who trust in a benevolent, all-knowing Father—is to wait patiently for God to reveal Himself. And reveal Himself He will. Always. But until God's perfect plan is made known, we must walk in faith and never lose hope. And we must continue to trust Him. Always.

No matter what we are going through, no matter how long the waiting for answers, of one thing we may be sure. God is faithful. He keeps His promises. What He starts, He finishes . . . including His perfect work in us.

Gloria Gaither

A PRAYER FOR GRACE

Dear Lord, Your wisdom is infinite, and the timing of Your Heavenly plan is perfect. You have a plan for my life that is grander than I can imagine. When I am impatient, remind me that You are never early or late. You are always on time, Father, so let me trust in You. Amen

TRUSTING GOD'S WILL

Teach me to do Your will, for You are my God; Your Spirit is good. Lead me in the land of uprightness.
—Psalm 143:10 NKJV

The Book of Judges tells the story of Deborah, the fearless woman who helped lead the army of Israel to victory over the Canaanites. Deborah was a judge and a prophetess, a woman called by God to lead her people. And when she answered God's call, she was rewarded with one of the great victories of Old Testament times.

Like Deborah, all of us are called to serve our Creator. And, like Deborah, we may sometimes find ourselves facing trials that can bring trembling to the very depths of our souls. As believers, we must seek God's will and follow it. When we do, we are rewarded with victories, some great and some small. When we entrust our lives to Him completely and without reservation, He gives us the strength to meet any challenge, the courage to face any trial, and the wisdom to live in His righteousness and in His peace.

The only safe place is in the center of God's will. It is not only the safest place. It is also the most rewarding and the most satisfying place to be.

Gigi Graham Tchividjian

I believe that in every time and place it is within our power to acquiesce in the will of God—and what peace it brings to do so!

Elisabeth Elliot

A PRAYER FOR GRACE

Lord, let Your will be my will. When I am confused, give me maturity and wisdom. When I am worried, give me courage and strength. Let me be Your faithful servant, Father, always seeking Your guidance and Your will for my life. Amen

THE VALUE OF WORK

Therefore by their fruits you will know them.

—Matthew 7:20 NKJV

God's Word teaches us the value of hard work. In his second letter to the Thessalonians, Paul warns, "if any would not work, neither should he eat" (3:10 KJV). And the Book of Proverbs proclaims, "One who is slack in his work is brother to one who destroys" (18:9 NIV). In short, God has created a world in which diligence is rewarded but sloth is not. So, whatever it is that you choose to do, do it with commitment, excitement, and vigor.

Hard work is not simply a proven way to get ahead, it's also part of God's plan for you. God did not create you for a life of mediocrity; He created you for far greater things. Reaching for greater things usually requires work and lots of it, which is perfectly fine with God. After all, He knows that you're up to the task, and He has big plans for you if you possess a loving heart and willing hands.

In the very place where God has put us, whatever its limitations, whatever kind of work it may be, we may indeed serve the Lord Christ.

Elisabeth Elliot

If you honor God with your work, He will honor you because of your work.

Marie T. Freeman

God provides the ingredients for our daily bread but expects us to do the baking. With our own hands!

Barbara Johnson

A PRAYER FOR GRACE

Heavenly Father, I seek to be Your faithful servant. When I am tired, give me strength. When I become frustrated, give me patience. When I lose sight of Your purpose for my life, give me a passion for my daily responsibilities, and when I have completed my work, let all the honor and glory be Yours. Amen

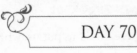

HIS GRACE IS SUFFICIENT

My grace is sufficient for you, for My strength is made perfect in weakness.

—2 Corinthians 12:9 NKJV

Of this you can be sure: the loving heart of God is sufficient to meet your needs. Whatever dangers you may face, whatever heartbreaks you must endure, God is with you, and He stands ready to comfort you and to heal you.

The Psalmist writes, "Weeping may endure for a night, but joy comes in the morning" (Psalm 30:5 NKJV). But when we are suffering, the morning may seem very far away. It is not. God promises that He is "near to those who have a broken heart" (Psalm 34:18 NKJV). In times of intense sadness, we must turn to Him, and we must encourage our friends and family members to do likewise.

If you are experiencing the intense pain of a recent loss, or if you are still mourning a loss from long ago, perhaps you are now ready to begin the next stage of your journey with God. If so, be mindful of this fact: the loving heart of God is sufficient to meet any challenge, including yours. Trust the sufficient heart of God.

Snuggle in God's arms. When you are hurting, when you feel lonely or left out, let Him cradle you, comfort you, reassure you of His all-sufficient power and love.

Kay Arthur

A PRAYER FOR GRACE

Dear Lord, You are sufficient for my needs, and I praise You. I will turn to You when I am fearful or worried. You are my loving heavenly Father, sufficient in all things and I will always trust You. Amen

SIMPLICITY NOW

But godliness with contentment is a great gain. For we brought nothing into the world, and we can take nothing out. But if we have food and clothing, we will be content with these. But those who want to be rich fall into temptation, a trap, and many foolish and harmful desires, which plunge people into ruin and destruction.

—1 Timothy 6:6-9 HCSB

Y ou live in a world where simplicity is in short supply. Think for a moment about the complexity of your everyday life and compare it to the lives of your ancestors. Certainly, you are the beneficiary of many technological innovations, but those innovations have a price: in all likelihood, your world is highly complex. Consider the following:

1. From the moment you wake up in the morning until the time you lay your head on the pillow at night, you are the target of an endless stream of advertising information. Each message is intended to grab your attention in order to

convince you to purchase things you didn't know you needed (and probably don't!).

2. Essential aspects of your life, including personal matters such as health care, are subject to an ever-increasing flood of rules and regulations.

3. Unless you take firm control of your time and your life, you may be overwhelmed by an ever-increasing tidal wave of complexity that threatens your happiness.

Your Heavenly Father understands the joy of living simply, and so should you. So do yourself a favor: keep your life as simple as possible. Simplicity is, indeed, genius. By simplifying your life, you are destined to improve it.

A PRAYER FOR GRACE

Dear Lord, help me understand the joys of simplicity. Life is complicated enough without my adding to the confusion. Wherever I happen to be, help me to keep it simple—very simple. Amen

THE POWER OF PERSEVERANCE

If you do nothing in a difficult time, your strength is limited.

—Proverbs 24:10 HCSB

I n a world filled with roadblocks and stumbling blocks, we need strength, courage, and perseverance. And, as an example of perfect perseverance, we need look no further than our Savior, Jesus Christ.

Jesus finished what He began. Despite the torture He endured, despite the shame of the cross, Jesus was steadfast in His faithfulness to God. We, too, must remain faithful, especially during times of hardship.

Perhaps you are in a hurry for God to reveal His plans for your life. If so, be forewarned: God operates on His own timetable, not yours. Sometimes, God may answer your prayers with silence, and when He does, you must patiently persevere. In times of trouble, you must remain steadfast and trust in the merciful goodness of your Heavenly Father. Whatever your problem, He can handle it. Your job is to keep persevering until He does.

Are you a Christian? If you are, how can you be hopeless? Are you so depressed by the greatness of your problems that you have given up all hope? Instead of giving up, would you patiently endure? Would you focus on Christ until you are so preoccupied with him alone that you fall prostrate before him?

Anne Graham Lotz

A PRAYER FOR GRACE

Lord, when life is difficult, I am tempted to abandon hope in the future. But You are my God, and I can draw strength from You. Let me trust You, Father, in good times and in bad times. Let me persevere—even if my soul is troubled—and let me follow Your Son, Jesus Christ, this day and forever. Amen

THE CORNERSTONE

The Lord is the strength of my life.

—Psalm 27:1 KJV

Have you made God the cornerstone of your life, or is He relegated to a few hours on Sunday morning? Have you genuinely allowed God to reign over every corner of your heart, or have you attempted to place Him in a spiritual compartment? The answer to these questions will determine the direction of your day and your life.

God loves you. In times of trouble, He will comfort you; in times of sorrow, He will dry your tears. When you are weak or sorrowful, God is as near as your next breath. He stands at the door of your heart and waits. Welcome Him in and allow Him to rule. And then, accept the peace, and the strength, and the protection, and the abundance that only God can give.

God walks with us. He scoops us up in His arms or simply sits with us in silent strength until we cannot avoid the awesome recognition that yes, even now, He is here.

Gloria Gaither

Measure the size of the obstacles against the size of God.

Beth Moore

So rejoice! You are giving Him what He asks you to give Him—the chance to show you what He can do.

Amy Carmichael

A Prayer for Grace

Lord, You have promised never to leave me or forsake me. You are always with me, protecting me and encouraging me. Whatever this day may bring, I thank You for Your love and for Your strength. Let me lean upon You, Father, this day and forever. Amen

THE LIGHT
OF THE WORLD

I have come as a light into the world, so that everyone who believes in Me would not remain in darkness.

—John 12:46 HCSB

The Bible says that you are "the light that gives light to the world." The Bible also says that you should live in a way that lets other people understand what it means to be a follower of Jesus.

What kind of light have you been giving off? Hopefully, you've been a good example for everybody to see. Why? Because the world needs all the light it can get, and that includes your light, too!

The old familiar hymn begins, "What a friend we have in Jesus . . . ." No truer words were ever penned. Jesus is the sovereign Friend and ultimate Savior of mankind. Christ showed enduring love for you by willingly sacrificing His own life so that you might have eternal life. As

a response to His sacrifice, you should love Him, praise Him, and share His message of salvation with your neighbors and with the world.

Do you seek to be an extreme follower of Christ? Then you must let your light shine . . . today and every day.

If we guard some corner of darkness in ourselves, we will soon be drawing someone else into darkness, shutting them out from the light in the face of Jesus Christ.

Elisabeth Elliot

A Prayer for Grace

Heavenly Father, I praise You for Your Son Jesus, the light of the world and my personal Savior. Let me share His Good News with all who cross my path, and let me share His love with all who need His healing touch. Amen

THE POWER OF PRAYER

*Don't worry about anything, but in everything,
through prayer and petition with thanksgiving, let
your requests be made known to God.*

—Philippians 4:6 HCSB

"The power of prayer": these words are
so familiar, yet sometimes we forget
what they mean. Prayer is a powerful
tool for communicating with our Creator; it is an
opportunity to commune with the Giver of all
things good. Prayer helps us find strength for today and hope for the future. Prayer is not a thing
to be taken lightly or to be used infrequently.

Is prayer an integral part of your daily life,
or is it a hit-or-miss habit? Do you "pray without
ceasing," or is your prayer life an afterthought?

The quality of your spiritual life will be in direct proportion to the quality of your prayer life.
Prayer changes things, and it changes you. Today,
instead of worrying about your next decision, ask
God to lead the way. Don't limit your prayers to
meals or to bedtime. Pray constantly about things

great and small. God is listening, and He wants to hear from you now.

When the Holy Spirit comes to dwell within us, I believe we gain a built-in inclination to take our concerns and needs to the Lord in prayer.

Shirley Dobson

What God gives in answer to our prayers will always be the thing we most urgently need, and it will always be sufficient.

Elisabeth Elliot

A PRAYER FOR GRACE

Dear Lord, make me a woman of constant prayer. Your Holy Word commands me to pray without ceasing. In all things great and small, at all times, whether happy or sad, let me seek Your wisdom and Your strength . . . in prayer. Amen

HE FORGIVES US

But God, who is abundant in mercy, because of His great love that He had for us, made us alive with the Messiah even though we were dead in trespasses. By grace you are saved!

—Ephesians 2:4-5 HCSB

ll of us have sinned. Sometimes our sins result from our own stubborn rebellion against God's commandments. And sometimes, we are swept up in events that are beyond our abilities to control. Under either set of circumstances, we may experience intense feelings of guilt. But God has an answer for the guilt that we feel. That answer, of course, is His forgiveness. When we confess our wrongdoings and repent from them, we are forgiven by the One who created us.

Are you troubled by feelings of guilt or regret? If so, you must repent from your misdeeds, and you must ask your Heavenly Father for His forgiveness. When you do so, He will forgive you completely and without reservation. Then, you must forgive yourself just as God has forgiven you: thoroughly and unconditionally.

Satan wants you to feel guilty. Your heavenly Father wants you to know that you are forgiven.

Warren Wiersbe

Even in long-term grief there is a way to bring closure and to rise above the rage, the guilt, the pain. In Christ this is possible.

Barbara Johnson

A PRAYER FOR GRACE

Dear Lord, thank You for the guilt that I feel when I disobey You. Help me confess my wrongdoings, help me accept Your forgiveness, and help me renew my passion to serve You. Amen

PLEASING GOD

The person who knows my commandments and keeps them, that's who loves me. And the person who loves me will be loved by my Father, and I will love him and make myself plain to him.

—John 14:21 MSG

When God made you, He equipped you with an array of talents and abilities that are uniquely yours. It's up to you to discover those talents and to use them, but sometimes the world will encourage you to do otherwise. At times, society will attempt to cubbyhole you, to standardize you, and to make you fit into a particular, preformed mold. Perhaps God has other plans.

Sometimes, because you're an imperfect human being, you may become so wrapped up in meeting society's expectations that you fail to focus on God's expectations. To do so is a mistake of major proportions—don't make it. Instead, seek God's guidance as you focus your energies on becoming the best "you" that you can possibly be. And, when it comes to matters of conscience, seek approval not from your peers, but from your Creator.

Whom will you try to please today: God or man? Your primary obligation is not to please imperfect men and women. Your obligation is to strive diligently to meet the expectations of an all-knowing and perfect God. Trust Him always. Love Him always. Praise Him always. And seek to please Him. Always.

Get ready for God to show you not only His pleasure, but His approval.

Joni Eareckson Tada

A Prayer for Grace

Dear Lord, today I will honor You with my thoughts, my actions, and my prayers. I will seek to please You, and I will strive to serve You. Your blessings are as limitless as Your love. And because I have been so richly blessed, I will worship You, Father, with thanksgiving in my heart and praise on my lips, this day and forever. Amen

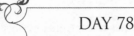
SHARING THE GOOD NEWS

Then He said to them, "Go into all the world and preach the gospel to the whole creation."

—Mark 16:15 HCSB

After His resurrection, Jesus addressed His disciples:

But the eleven disciples proceeded to Galilee, to the mountain which Jesus had designated. When they saw Him, they worshiped Him; but some were doubtful. And Jesus came up and spoke to them, saying, "All authority has been given to Me in heaven and on earth. Go therefore and make disciples of all the nations, baptizing them in the name of the Father and the Son and the Holy Spirit, teaching them to observe all that I commanded you; and lo, I am with you always, even to the end of the age" (Matthew 28:16–20 NASB).

Christ's great commission applies to Christians of every generation, including our own. Jesus commanded His disciples to become fishers of men. We must do likewise, and we must do so today. Tomorrow may indeed be too late.

Our commission is quite specific. We are told to be His witness to all nations. For us, as His disciples, to refuse any part of this commission frustrates the love of Jesus Christ, the Son of God.

Catherine Marshall

A PRAYER FOR GRACE

Heavenly Father, every man and woman, every boy and girl is Your child. You desire that all Your children know Jesus as their Lord and Savior. Father, let me be part of Your Great Commission. Let me give, let me pray, and let me go out into this world so that I might be a fisher of men . . . for You. Amen

REAL REPENTANCE

There will be more joy in heaven over one sinner who repents than over 99 righteous people who don't need repentance.

—Luke 15:7 HCSB

Who among us has sinned? All of us. But, God calls upon us to turn away from sin by following His commandments. And the good news is this: When we do ask for God's forgiveness and turn our hearts to Him, He forgives us absolutely and completely.

Genuine repentance requires more than simply offering God apologies for our misdeeds. Real repentance may start with feelings of sorrow and remorse, but it ends only when we turn away from the sin that has heretofore distanced us from our Creator. In truth, we offer our most meaningful apologies to God, not with our words, but with our actions. As long as we are still engaged in sin, we may be "repenting," but we have not fully "repented."

Is there an aspect of your life that is distancing you from your God? If so, ask for His forgiveness, and—just as importantly—stop sinning. Then, wrap yourself in the protection of God's Word. When you do, you will be secure.

When true repentance comes, God will not hesitate for a moment to forgive, cast the sins in the sea of forgetfulness, and put the child on the road to restoration.

Beth Moore

A PRAYER FOR GRACE

When I stray from Your commandments, Lord, I must not only confess my sins, I must also turn from them. When I fall short, help me to change. When I reject Your Word and Your will for my life, guide me back to Your side. Forgive my sins, Dear Lord, and help me live according to Your plan for my life. Your plan is perfect, Father; I am not. Let me trust in You. Amen

SETTING THE RIGHT EXAMPLE

You should be an example to the believers in speech, in conduct, in love, in faith, in purity.

—1 Timothy 4:12 HCSB

Whether we like it or not, all of us are role models. Our friends and family members watch our actions and, as followers of Christ, we are obliged to act accordingly.

What kind of example are you? Are you the kind of woman whose life serves as a genuine example of righteousness? Are you a woman whose behavior serves as a positive role model for young people? Are you the kind of woman whose actions, day in and day out, are based upon kindness, faithfulness, and a love for the Lord? If so, you are not only blessed by God, but you are also a powerful force for good in a world that desperately needs positive influences such as yours.

Corrie ten Boom advised, "Don't worry about what you do not understand. Worry about what you do understand in the Bible but do not live by." And that's sound advice because our families and friends are watching . . . and so, for that matter, is God.

In your desire to share the gospel, you may be the only Jesus someone else will ever meet. Be real and be involved with people.

Barbara Johnson

The religion of Jesus Christ has an ethical as well as a doctrinal side.

Lottie Moon

A PRAYER FOR GRACE

Lord, make me a worthy example to my family and friends. And, let my words and my deeds serve as a testimony to the changes You have made in my life. I will praise You, Father, by following in the footsteps of Your Son so that others may see Him through me. Amen

FOCUSING ON GOD, NOT FEAR

But He said to them, "Why are you fearful, O you of little faith?" Then He arose and rebuked the winds and the sea, and there was a great calm.

—Matthew 8:26 NKJV

A frightening storm rose quickly on the Sea of Galilee, and the disciples were afraid. Because of their limited faith, they feared for their lives. When they turned to Jesus, He calmed the waters and He rebuked His disciples for their lack of faith in Him.

On occasion, we, like the disciples, are frightened by the inevitable storms of life. Why are we afraid? Because we, like the disciples, possess imperfect faith.

When we genuinely accept God's promises as absolute truth, when we trust Him with life-here-on-earth and life eternal, we have little to fear. Faith in God is the antidote to worry. Faith in God is the foundation of courage and the source of power. Today, let us trust God more completely and, by doing so, move beyond our fears to a place of abundance, assurance, and peace.

Fear is a self-imposed prison that will keep you from becoming what God intends for you to be.

Rick Warren

His hand on me is a father's hand, gently guiding and encouraging. His hand lets me know he is with me, so I am not afraid.

Mary Morrison Suggs

A PRAYER FOR GRACE

Father, even when I walk through the valley of the shadow of death, I will fear no evil because You are with me. Thank You, Lord, for Your perfect love, a love that casts out fear and gives me strength and courage to meet the challenges of this world. Amen

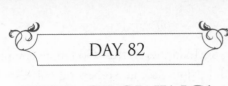

KEEP GROWING!

Dear brothers and sisters, whenever trouble comes your way, let it be an opportunity for joy. For when your faith is tested, your endurance has a chance to grow. So let it grow, for when your endurance is fully developed, you will be strong in character and ready for anything.

—James 1:2-4 NLT

If you are to grow as a woman, you need both knowledge and wisdom. Knowledge is found in textbooks. Wisdom, on the other hand, is found through experience, through years of trial and error, and through careful attention to the Word of God. Knowledge is an important building block in a well-lived life, and it pays rich dividends both personally and professionally. But, wisdom is even more important because it refashions not only your mind, but also your heart.

When it comes to your faith, God doesn't intend for you to stand still. He wants you to keep growing as a woman and as a spiritual being. No matter how "grown-up" you may be, you still have growing to do. And the more you grow, the more lovely you become, inside and out.

Growth in depth and strength and consistency and fruitfulness and ultimately in Christlikeness is only possible when the winds of life are contrary to personal comfort.

Anne Graham Lotz

You cannot grow spiritually until you have the assurance that Christ is in your life.

Vonette Bright

A PRAYER FOR GRACE

Dear Lord, when I open my heart to You, I am blessed. Today, I will praise You, Father, as I accept Your love and Your wisdom. And, I will do my best to continue to grow in my faith every day that I live. Amen

CELEBRATING HIS GIFTS

Rejoice in the Lord always. I will say it again: Rejoice!
—Philippians 4:4 HCSB

The 100th Psalm reminds us that the entire earth should "Shout for joy to the Lord." As God's children, we are blessed beyond measure, but sometimes, as busy women living in a demanding world, we are slow to count our gifts and even slower to give thanks to the Giver.

Our blessings include life and health, family and friends, freedom and possessions—for starters. And, the gifts we receive from God are multiplied when we share them. May we always give thanks to God for His blessings, and may we always demonstrate our gratitude by sharing our gifts with others.

The 118th Psalm reminds us that, "This is the day which the LORD has made; let us rejoice and be glad in it" (v. 24, NASB). May we celebrate this day and the One who created it.

Joy is a by-product not of happy circumstances, education or talent, but of a healthy relationship with God and a determination to love Him no matter what.

Barbara Johnson

God knows everything. He can manage everything, and He loves us. Surely this is enough for a fullness of joy that is beyond words.

Hannah Whitall Smith

A PRAYER FOR GRACE

Lord God, You have created a grand and glorious universe that is far beyond human understanding. The heavens proclaim Your handiwork, and every star in the sky tells of Your power. Let me celebrate You and Your marvelous creation, Father, and let me give thanks for this day. Today is Your gift to me, Lord. Let me use it to Your glory while giving all the praise to You. Amen

HE BLESSES
THE RIGHTEOUS

The LORD approves of those who are good, but he condemns those who plan wickedness.

—Proverbs 12:2 NLT

If you want to know God, you should obey God. But obeying Him isn't always easy. You live in a world that presents countless temptations to stray far from God's path. So here's some timely advice: when you're confronted with sin, walk—or better yet run—in the opposite direction.

When you seek righteousness for yourself—and when you seek the companionship of people who do likewise—you will reap the spiritual rewards that God has in store for you. When you live in accordance with God's commandments, you will be blessed. When you genuinely seek to follow in the footsteps of God's Son, you will experience God's presence, God's peace, and God's abundance.

So make yourself this promise: Support only those activities that further God's kingdom and your own spiritual growth. Then, prepare to reap the blessings that God has promised to all those who live according to His will and His Word.

Holiness has never been the driving force of the majority. It is, however, mandatory for anyone who wants to enter the kingdom.

Elisabeth Elliot

A Prayer for Grace

Holy, Holy, Holy . . . You are a righteous and holy God, and You have called me to be Your righteous servant. When I fall short, forgive me, Father, and renew a spirit of holiness within me. Lead me, Lord, along Your path, and guide me far from the temptations of this world. Let Your Holy Word guide my actions, and let Your love reside in my heart, this day and every day. Amen

ENCOURAGING WORDS

I want their hearts to be encouraged and joined together in love, so that they may have all the riches of assured understanding, and have the knowledge of God's mystery—Christ.

—Colossians 2:2 HCSB

Are you a woman who is a continuing source of encouragement to your family and friends? Hopefully so. After all, one of the reasons that God put you here is to serve and encourage other people—starting with the people who live under your roof.

In his letter to the Ephesians, Paul writes, "Do not let any unwholesome talk come out of your mouths, but only what is helpful for building others up according to their needs, that it may benefit those who listen" (4:29 NIV). This passage reminds us that, as Christians, we are instructed to choose our words carefully so as to build others up through wholesome, honest encouragement. How can we build others up? By celebrating their victories and their accomplishments. As the old saying goes, "When someone does something good, applaud—you'll make two people happy."

Today, look for the good in others and celebrate the good that you find. When you do, you'll be a powerful force of encouragement in your corner of the world . . . and a worthy servant to your God.

True friends will always lift you higher and challenge you to walk in a manner pleasing to our Lord.

Lisa Bevere

A PRAYER FOR GRACE

Dear Lord, because I am Your child, I am blessed. You have loved me eternally, cared for me faithfully, and saved me through the gift of Your Son Jesus. Just as You have lifted me up, Lord, let me also lift up others in a spirit of encouragement and hope. And, if I can help even a single person, Lord, may the glory be Yours. Amen

HAVE A REGULAR APPOINTMENT WITH GOD

But have nothing to do with irreverent and silly myths. Rather, train yourself in godliness.

—1 Timothy 4:7 HCSB

Each new day is a gift from God, and if we are wise, we will spend a few quiet moments each morning thanking the Giver. Daily life is woven together with the threads of habit, and no habit is more important to our spiritual health than the discipline of daily prayer and devotion to the Creator.

When we begin each day with heads bowed and hearts lifted, we remind ourselves of God's love, His protection, and His commandments. And if we are wise, we align our priorities for the coming day with the teachings and commandments that God has given us through His Word.

Are you seeking to change some aspect of your life? Do you seek to improve the condition of your spiritual or physical health? If so, ask for God's help and ask for it many times each day . . . starting with your morning devotional.

Jesus challenges you and me to keep our focus daily on the cross of His will if we want to be His disciples.

Anne Graham Lotz

A person with no devotional life generally struggles with faith and obedience.

Charles Stanley

A PRAYER FOR GRACE

Dear Lord, I want to understand Your direction for my life. When I find quiet moments, I will pray, and I will study Your Word. And, as I go about my daily activities, I will try to say things and do things that are pleasing to You. Amen

YOUR POTENTIAL

Have faith in the Lord your God, and you will stand strong. Have faith in his prophets, and you will succeed.

—2 Chronicles 20:20 NCV

Do you expect your future to be bright? Are you willing to dream king-sized dreams . . . and are you willing to work diligently to make those dreams happen? Hopefully so—after all, God promises that we can do "all things" through Him. Yet most of us live far below our potential. We take half measures; we dream small dreams; we waste precious time and energy on the distractions of the world. But God has other plans for us.

In her diary, Anne Frank wrote, "The good news is that you really don't know how great you can be, how much you can love, what you can accomplish, and what your potential is." These words apply to you. You possess great potential, potential that you must use or forfeit. And the time to fulfill that potential is now.

Freedom from the rule of sin releases the potential for which we were created—to reflect the glory of the Glorious One.

Susan Hunt

If you want to reach your potential, you need to add a strong work ethic to your talent.

John Maxwell

A Prayer for Grace

Lord, You have blessed me with a love that is far beyond my limited understanding. You loved me before I was ever born; You sent Your Son Jesus to redeem me from my sins; You have given me the gift of eternal life. And, You have given me special talents; let me use those talents to the best of my ability and to the glory of Your kingdom so that I might be a good and faithful servant this day and forever. Amen

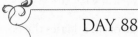

YOUR REASONS
TO REJOICE

Set your minds on what is above, not on what is on the earth.

—Colossians 3:2 HCSB

The Christian life is a cause for celebration, but sometimes we don't feel much like celebrating. In fact, when the weight of the world seems to bear down upon our shoulders, celebration may be the last thing on our minds . . . but it shouldn't be. As God's children, we are all blessed beyond measure on good days and bad. This day is a non-renewable resource—once it's gone, it's gone forever. We should give thanks for this day while using it for the glory of God.

What will be your attitude today? Will you be fearful, angry, bored, or worried? Will you be cynical, bitter, or pessimistic? If so, God wants to have a little talk with you.

God created you in His own image, and He wants you to experience joy and abundance. But,

God will not force His joy upon you; you must claim it for yourself. So today, and every day hereafter, celebrate the life that God has given you. Think optimistically about yourself and your future. Give thanks to the One who has given you everything, and trust in your heart that He wants to give you so much more.

Each one of us is responsible for our own happiness. If we choose to allow ourselves to become miserable and unhappy, the problem is ours, not someone else's.

Joyce Meyer

A PRAYER FOR GRACE

Lord, I pray for an attitude that is Christlike. Whatever my situation, whether good or bad, happy or sad, let me respond with an attitude of optimism, faith, and love for You. Amen

THE BEST POLICY

Therefore, putting away lying, "Let each one of you speak truth with his neighbor," for we are members of one another.

—Ephesians 4:25 NKJV

It has been said on many occasions and in many ways that honesty is the best policy. For believers, it is far more important to note that honesty is God's policy. And if we are to be servants worthy of our Savior, Jesus Christ, we must be honest and forthright in our communications with others.

Sometimes, honesty is difficult; sometimes, honesty is painful; always, honesty is God's commandment. In the Book of Exodus, God did not command, "Thou shalt not bear false witness when it is convenient." And He didn't say, "Thou shalt not bear false witness most of the time." God said, "Thou shalt not bear false witness against thy neighbor." Period.

Sometime soon, perhaps even today, you will be tempted to bend the truth or perhaps even to break it. Resist that temptation. Truth is God's way…and it must also be yours. Period.

The single most important element in any human relationship is honesty—with oneself, with God, and with others.

Catherine Marshall

A person who really cares about his or her neighbor, a person who genuinely loves others, is a person who bears witness to the truth.

Anne Graham Lotz

A PRAYER FOR GRACE

Lord, You are a God of truth; let me be a woman of truth. Sometimes speaking the truth is difficult, but when I am weak or fearful, Lord, give me the strength to speak words that are worthy of the One who created me, so that others might see Your eternal truth reflected in my words and my deeds. Amen

THE POISON OF ENVY

We must not become conceited, provoking one another, envying one another.

—Galatians 5:26 HCSB

Because we are frail, imperfect human beings, we are sometimes envious of others. But God's Word warns us that envy is sin. Thus, we must guard ourselves against the natural tendency to feel resentment and jealousy when other people experience good fortune.

As believers, we have absolutely no reason to be envious of any people on earth. After all, as Christians we are already recipients of the greatest gift in all creation: God's grace. We have been promised the gift of eternal life through God's only begotten Son, and we must count that gift as our most precious possession.

Rather than succumbing to the sin of envy, we should focus on the marvelous things that God has done for us—starting with Christ's sacrifice. And we must refrain from preoccupying ourselves with the blessings that God has chosen to give others.

So here's a surefire formula for a happier, healthier life: Count your own blessings and let your neighbors count theirs. It's the godly way to live.

Instead of allowing the pain in our lives to shape our character, taking us through rivers of humility and brokenness, we can let the sorrow become overwhelming, choking out life, filling us instead with bitterness and resentment.

Angela Thomas

A PRAYER FOR GRACE

Dear Lord, You are the Giver of all good gifts. Today I will praise You for my blessings, and I won't be envious of the blessings You've given to others. Amen

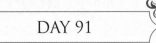

HIS TRUTH

You will know the truth, and the truth will set you free.

—John 8:32 HCSB

God is vitally concerned with truth. His Word teaches the truth; His Spirit reveals the truth; His Son leads us to the truth. When we open our hearts to God, and when we allow His Son to rule over our thoughts and our lives, God reveals Himself, and we come to understand the truth about ourselves and the Truth (with a capital T) about God's gift of grace.

The familiar words of John 8:32 remind us that when we come to know God's Truth, we are liberated. Have you been liberated by that Truth? And are you living in accordance with the eternal truths that you find in God's Holy Word? Hopefully so.

Today, as you fulfill the responsibilities that God has placed before you, ask yourself this question: "Do my thoughts and actions bear witness to the ultimate Truth that God has placed in my heart, or am I allowing the pressures of everyday life to overwhelm me?" It's a profound question that deserves an answer . . . now.

The Holy Spirit was given to guide us into all truth, but He doesn't do it all at once.

Elisabeth Elliot

To worship Him in truth means to worship Him honestly, without hypocrisy, standing open and transparent before Him.

Anne Graham Lotz

A PRAYER FOR GRACE

Heavenly Father, You are the way and the truth and the light. Today—as I follow Your way and share Your Good News—let me be a worthy example to others and a worthy servant to You. Amen

HIS DISCIPLE

He has told you men what is good and what it is the Lord requires of you: Only to act justly, to love faithfulness, and to walk humbly with your God.

—Micah 6:8 HCSB

When Jesus addressed His disciples, He warned that each one must "take up his cross and follow Me." The disciples must have known exactly what the Master meant. In Jesus' day, prisoners were forced to carry their own crosses to the location where they would be put to death. Thus, Christ's message was clear: in order to follow Him, Christ's disciples must deny themselves and, instead, trust Him completely. Nothing has changed since then.

If we are to be disciples of Christ, we must trust Him and place Him at the very center of our beings. Jesus never comes "next." He is always first. The paradox, of course, is that only by sacrificing ourselves to Him do we gain salvation for ourselves.

Do you seek to be a worthy disciple of Christ? Then pick up His cross today and every day that you live. When you do, He will bless you now and forever.

Be filled with the Holy Spirit; join a church where the members believe the Bible and know the Lord; seek the fellowship of other Christians; learn and be nourished by God's Word and His many promises. Conversion is not the end of your journey—it is only the beginning.

Corrie ten Boom

A PRAYER FOR GRACE

Help me, Lord, to understand what cross I am to bear this day. Give me the strength and the courage to carry that cross along the path of Your choosing so that I may be a worthy disciple of Your Son. Amen

CHEERFUL GENEROSITY

So let each one give as he purposes in his heart, not grudgingly or of necessity; for God loves a cheerful giver.

—2 Corinthians 9:7 NKJV

The thread of generosity is woven—completely and inextricably—into the very fabric of Christ's teachings. As He sent His disciples out to heal the sick and spread God's message of salvation, Jesus offered this guiding principle: "Freely you have received, freely give" (Matthew 10:8 NIV). The principle still applies. If we are to be disciples of Christ, we must give freely of our time, our possessions, and our love.

Lisa Whelchel spoke for Christian women everywhere when she observed, "The Lord has abundantly blessed me all of my life. I'm not trying to pay Him back for all of His wonderful gifts; I just realize that He gave them to me to give away." All of us have been blessed, and all of us are called to share those blessings without reservation.

Today, make this pledge and keep it: Be a cheerful, generous, courageous giver. The world needs your help, and you need the spiritual rewards that will be yours when you share your possessions, your talents, and your time.

We can't do everything, but can we do anything more valuable than invest ourselves in another?

Elisabeth Elliot

The measure of a life, after all, is not its duration but its donation.

Corrie ten Boom

A PRAYER FOR GRACE

Lord, You have been so generous with me; let me be generous with others. Help me to give generously of my time and my possessions as I care for those in need. And, make me a humble giver, Lord, so that all the glory and the praise might be Yours. Amen

PUTTING GOD FIRST

You shall have no other gods before Me.

—Exodus 20:3 NKJV

As you think about the nature of your relationship with God, remember this: you will always have some type of relationship with Him—it is inevitable that your life must be lived in relationship to God. The question is not if you will have a relationship with Him; the burning question is whether that relationship will be one that seeks to honor Him . . . or not.

Are you willing to place God first in your life? And, are you willing to welcome God's Son into your heart? Unless you can honestly answer these questions with a resounding yes, then your relationship with God isn't what it could be or should be. Thankfully, God is always available, He's always ready to forgive, and He's waiting to hear from you now. The rest, of course, is up to you.

I lived with Indians who made pots out of clay which they used for cooking. Nobody was interested in the pot. Everybody was interested in what was inside. The same clay taken out of the same riverbed, always made in the same design, nothing special about it. Well, I'm a clay pot, and let me not forget it. But, the excellency of the power is of God and not us.

Elisabeth Elliot

Make God's will the focus of your life day by day. If you seek to please Him and Him alone, you'll find yourself satisfied with life.

Kay Arthur

A PRAYER FOR GRACE

Dear Lord, Your love is eternal and Your laws are everlasting. When I obey Your commandments, I am blessed. Today, I invite You to reign over every corner of my heart. I will have faith in You, Father. I will sense Your presence; I will accept Your love; I will trust Your will; and I will praise You for the Savior of my life: Your Son Jesus. Amen

FOLLOWING CHRIST

But whoever keeps His word, truly in him the love of God is perfected. This is how we know we are in Him: the one who says he remains in Him should walk just as He walked.

—1 John 2:5-6 HCSB

J esus walks with you. Are you walking with Him? Hopefully, you will choose to walk with Him today and every day of your life.

Jesus loved you so much that He endured unspeakable humiliation and suffering for you. How will you respond to Christ's sacrifice? Will you take up His cross and follow Him (Luke 9:23), or will you choose another path? When you place your hopes squarely at the foot of the cross, when you place Jesus squarely at the center of your life, you will be blessed. If you seek to be a worthy disciple of Jesus, you must acknowledge that He never comes "next." He is always first.

Do you hope to fulfill God's purpose for your life? Do you seek a life of abundance and peace? Do you intend to be Christian not just in name, but in deed? Then follow Christ. Follow Him by picking up His cross today and every day that you live. When you do, you will quickly discover that Christ's love has the power to change everything, including you.

Will you, with a glad and eager surrender, hand yourself and all that concerns you over into his hands? If you will do this, your soul will begin to know something of the joy of union with Christ.

Hannah Whitall Smith

A Prayer for Grace

Dear Lord, You sent Your Son so that I might have abundant life and eternal life. I praise You, Father, for my Savior, Christ Jesus. I will follow Him, honor Him, and share His Good News, this day and every day. Amen

FORGIVENESS NOW

Be merciful, just as your Father also is merciful.

—Luke 6:36 HCSB

The world holds few if any rewards for those who remain angrily focused upon the past. Still, the act of forgiveness is difficult for all but the most saintly men and women. Are you mired in the quicksand of bitterness or regret? If so, you are not only disobeying God's Word, you are also wasting your time.

Being frail, fallible, imperfect human beings, most of us are quick to anger, quick to blame, slow to forgive, and even slower to forget. Yet as Christians, we are commanded to forgive others, just as we, too, have been forgiven.

If there exists even one person—alive or dead—against whom you hold bitter feelings, it's time to forgive. Or, if you are embittered against yourself for some past mistake or shortcoming, it's finally time to forgive yourself and move on. Hatred, bitterness, and regret are not part of God's plan for your life. Forgiveness is.

Forgiveness is actually the best revenge because it not only sets us free from the person we forgive, but it frees us to move into all that God has in store for us.

Stormie Omartian

God expects us to forgive others as He has forgiven us; we are to follow His example by having a forgiving heart.

Vonette Bright

God forgets the past. Imitate him.

Max Lucado

A PRAYER FOR GRACE

Dear Lord, You have forgiven me; let me show my thankfulness to You by offering forgiveness to others. Today, let forgiveness rule my heart, even when forgiveness is difficult. Let me be Your obedient servant, Lord, and let me be a woman who forgives others just as You have forgiven me. Amen

THE POWER OF YOUR THOUGHTS

Set your minds on what is above, not on what is on the earth.

—Colossians 3:2 HCSB

How will you direct your thoughts today? Will you dwell upon those things that are honorable, true, and worthy of praise (Philippians 4:8)? Or will you allow your thoughts to be hijacked by the negativity that seems to dominate our troubled world?

God intends that you be an ambassador for Him, an enthusiastic, hope-filled Christian. But God won't force you to adopt a positive attitude. It's up to you to do think positively about your blessings and opportunities . . . or not. So, today and every day hereafter, celebrate this life that God has given you by focusing your thoughts and your energies upon "things that are excellent and worthy of praise." Today, count your blessings instead of your hardships. And thank the Giver of all things good for gifts that are simply too numerous to count.

Attitude is the mind's paintbrush; it can color any situation.

Barbara Johnson

No matter how little we can change about our circumstances, we always have a choice about our attitude toward the situation.

Vonette Bright

A PRAYER FOR GRACE

Dear Lord, keep my thoughts focused on Your love, Your power, Your promises, and Your Son. When I am worried, I will turn to You for comfort; when I am weak, I will turn to You for strength; when I am troubled, I will turn to You for patience and perspective. Help me guard my thoughts, Father, so that I may honor You today and every day that I live. Amen

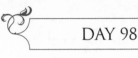

PRAISING HIM FOR THIS DAY

Teach us to number our days carefully so that we may develop wisdom in our hearts.

—Psalm 90:12 HCSB

This day is a gift from God. How will you use it? Will you celebrate God's gifts and obey His commandments? Will you share words of encouragement and hope with all who cross your path? Will you share the Good News of the risen Christ? Will you trust in the Father and praise His glorious handiwork? The answer to these questions will determine, to a surprising extent, the direction and the quality of your day.

The familiar words of Psalm 118:24 remind us of a profound yet simple truth: "This is the day which the LORD hath made; we will rejoice and be glad in it" (KJV). For Christian believers, every day begins and ends with God and His Son. Christ came to this earth to give us abundant life and eternal salvation. We give thanks to our

Maker when we treasure each day and use it to the fullest.

Today, may we give thanks for this day and for the One who created it.

Submit each day to God, knowing that He is God over all your tomorrows.

Kay Arthur

Every day of our lives we make choices about how we're going to live that day.

Luci Swindoll

A PRAYER FOR GRACE

Lord, You have given me another day of life; let me celebrate this day, and let me use it according to Your plan. I praise You, Father, for my life and for the friends and family members who make it rich. Enable me to live each moment to the fullest as I give thanks for Your creation, for Your love, and for Your Son. Amen

TRUST HIM

*The one who understands a matter finds success, and
the one who trusts in the Lord will be happy.*

—Proverbs 16:20 HCSB

Open your Bible to its center, and you'll
find the Book of Psalms. In it are some
of the most beautiful words ever trans-
lated into the English language, with none more
beautiful than the 23rd Psalm. David describes
God as being like a shepherd who cares for His
flock. No wonder these verses have provided
comfort and hope for generations of believers.

On occasion, you will confront circumstances that trouble you to the very core of your soul.
When you are afraid, trust in God. When you are
worried, turn your concerns over to Him. When
you are anxious, be still and listen for the quiet
assurance of God's promises. And then, place
your life in His hands. He is your Shepherd today
and throughout eternity. Trust the Shepherd.

The only safe place is in the center of God's will. It is not only the safest place. It is also the most rewarding and the most satisfying place to be.

Gigi Graham Tchividjian

The center of power is not to be found in summit meetings or in peace conferences. It is not in Peking or Washington or the United Nations, but rather where a child of God prays in the power of the Spirit for God's will to be done in her life, in her home, and in the world around her.

Ruth Bell Graham

A PRAYER FOR GRACE

Lord, when I trust in things of this earth, I will be disappointed. But, when I put my faith in You, I am secure. You are my rock and my shield. Upon Your firm foundation I will build my life. When I am worried, Lord, let me trust in You. You will love me and protect me, and You will share Your boundless grace today, tomorrow, and forever. Amen

THE PRICELESS GIFT OF ETERNAL LIFE

For God so loved the world that He gave His only begotten Son, that whoever believes in Him should not perish but have everlasting life.

—John 3:16 NKJV

Ours is not a distant God. Ours is a God who understands—far better than we ever could—the essence of what it means to be human. How marvelous it is that God became a man and walked among us. Had He not chosen to do so, we might feel removed from a distant Creator.

God understands our hopes, our fears, and our temptations. He understands what it means to be angry and what it costs to forgive. He knows the heart, the conscience, and the soul of every person who has ever lived, including you. And God has a plan of salvation that is intended for you. Accept it. Accept God's gift through the person of His Son Christ Jesus, and then rest assured: God walked among us so that you might have eternal life; amazing though it may seem, He did it for you.

I can still hardly believe it. I, with shriveled, bent fingers, atrophied muscles, gnarled knees, and no feeling from the shoulders down, will one day have a new body—light, bright and clothed in righteousness—powerful and dazzling.

Joni Eareckson Tada

A PRAYER FOR GRACE

Lord, I am only here on this earth for a brief while. But, You have offered me the priceless gift of eternal life through Your Son Jesus. I accept Your gift, Lord, with thanksgiving and praise. Let me share the good news of my salvation with those who need Your healing touch. Amen

More from God's Word about Peace

I leave you peace; my peace I give you. I do not give it to you as the world does. So don't let your hearts be troubled or afraid.

John 14:27 NCV

If your sinful nature controls your mind, there is death. But if the Holy Spirit controls your mind, there is life and peace.

Romans 8:6 NLT

If it is possible, as far as it depends on you, live at peace with everyone.

Romans 12:18 NIV

And the peace of God, which surpasses all understanding, will guard your hearts and minds through Christ Jesus. Finally, brethren, whatever things are true, whatever things are noble, whatever things are just, whatever things are pure, whatever things are lovely, whatever things are of good report, if there is any virtue and if there is anything praiseworthy—meditate on these things.

Philippians 4:7-8 NKJV

MORE FROM GOD'S WORD ABOUT SPIRITUAL GROWTH

For this reason also, since the day we heard this, we haven't stopped praying for you. We are asking that you may be filled with the knowledge of His will in all wisdom and spiritual understanding.

Colossians 1:9 HCSB

I want their hearts to be encouraged and joined together in love, so that they may have all the riches of assured understanding, and have the knowledge of God's mystery—Christ.

Colossians 2:2 HCSB

Run away from infantile indulgence. Run after mature righteousness—faith, love, peace—joining those who are in honest and serious prayer before God.

2 Timothy 2:22 MSG

Grow in grace and understanding of our Master and Savior, Jesus Christ. Glory to the Master, now and forever! Yes!

2 Peter 3:18 MSG

We also have joy with our troubles, because we know that these troubles produce patience. And patience produces character, and character produces hope.

Romans 5:3-4 NCV

The LORD also will be a stronghold for the oppressed, a stronghold in times of trouble.

Psalm 9:9 NASB

You pulled me from the brink of death, my feet from the cliff-edge of doom. Now I stroll at leisure with God in the sunlit fields of life.

Psalm 56:13 MSG

Don't fret or worry. Instead of worrying, pray. Let petitions and praises shape your worries into prayers, letting God know your concerns. Before you know it, a sense of God's wholeness, everything coming together for good, will come and settle you down. It's wonderful what happens when Christ displaces worry at the center of your life.

Philippians 4:6-7 MSG

MORE FROM GOD'S WORD ABOUT CONTENTMENT

I have learned to be content in whatever circumstances I am.

Philippians 4:11 HCSB

The LORD will give strength to His people; the LORD will bless His people with peace.

Psalm 29:11 NKJV

How priceless is your unfailing love! Both high and low among men find refuge in the shadow of your wings. They feast on the abundance of your house; you give them drink from your river of delights. For with you is the fountain of life; in your light we see light.

Psalm 36:7-9 NIV

Let your conduct be without covetousness; be content with such things as you have. For He Himself has said, "I will never leave you nor forsake you."

Hebrews 13:5 NKJV

More from God's Word about Strength

And He said to me, "My grace is sufficient for you, for My strength is made perfect in weakness."

2 Corinthians 12:9 NKJV

You, therefore, my child, be strong in the grace that is in Christ Jesus.

2 Timothy 2:1 HCSB

The Lord is my strength and my song; He has become my salvation.

Exodus 15:2 HCSB

He gives strength to the weary and strengthens the powerless.

Isaiah 40:29 HCSB

But those who wait on the Lord shall renew their strength; they shall mount up with wings like eagles, they shall run and not be weary, they shall walk and not faint.

Isaiah 40:31 NKJV

More from God's Word about Success

Success, success to you, and success to those who help you, for your God will help you....

1 Chronicles 12:18 NIV

But as for you, be strong and do not give up, for your work will be rewarded.

2 Chronicles 15:7 NIV

Let us not become weary in doing good, for at the proper time we will reap a harvest if we do not give up.

Galatians 6:9 NIV

You need to persevere so that when you have done the will of God, you will receive what he has promised.

Hebrews 10:36 NIV

The one who understands a matter finds success, and the one who trusts in the Lord will be happy.

Proverbs 16:20 HCSB

MORE FROM GOD'S WORD ABOUT COURAGE

But when Jesus heard it, He answered him, "Don't be afraid. Only believe."

Luke 8:50 HCSB

For God has not given us a spirit of fearfulness, but one of power, love, and sound judgment.

2 Timothy 1:7 HCSB

Be alert, stand firm in the faith, be brave and strong.

1 Corinthians 16:13 HCSB

But He said to them, "Why are you fearful, you of little faith?" Then He got up and rebuked the winds and the sea. And there was a great calm.

Matthew 8:26 HCSB

So do not fear, for I am with you; do not be dismayed, for I am your God. I will strengthen you and help you; I will uphold you with my righteous right hand.

Isaiah 41:10 NIV

MORE FROM GOD'S WORD ABOUT DECISIONS

I have set before you life and death, blessing and curse. Choose life so that you and your descendants may live, love the Lord your God, obey Him, and remain faithful to Him. For He is your life, and He will prolong your life in the land the Lord swore to give to your fathers Abraham, Isaac, and Jacob.

Deuteronomy 30:19-20 HCSB

Ignorant zeal is worthless; haste makes waste.

Proverbs 19:2 MSG

But Daniel purposed in his heart that he would not defile himself....

Daniel 1:8 KJV

But seek first the kingdom of God and His righteousness, and all these things will be provided for you.

Matthew 6:33 HCSB

Above all and before all, do this: Get Wisdom! Write this at the top of your list: Get Understanding!

Proverbs 4:7 MSG

More from God's Word about Abundance

Live in me. Make your home in me just as I do in you. In the same way that a branch can't bear grapes by itself but only by being joined to the vine, you can't bear fruit unless you are joined with me. I am the Vine, you are the branches. When you're joined with me and I with you, the relation intimate and organic, the harvest is sure to be abundant.

John 15:4-5 MSG

Until now you have asked for nothing in My name. Ask and you will receive, that your joy may be complete.

John 16:24 HCSB

Come to terms with God and be at peace; in this way good will come to you.

Job 22:21 HCSB

If you give, you will receive. Your gift will return to you in full measure, pressed down, shaken together to make room for more, and running over. Whatever measure you use in giving—large or small—it will be used to measure what is given back to you.

Luke 6:38 NLT

More from God's Word about Materialism

He who trusts in his riches will fall, but the righteous will flourish . . . .

Proverbs 11:28 NKJV

No one can serve two masters. The person will hate one master and love the other, or will follow one master and refuse to follow the other. You cannot serve both God and worldly riches.

Matthew 6:24 NCV

For the mind-set of the flesh is death, but the mind-set of the Spirit is life and peace.

Romans 8:6 HCSB

Since we entered the world penniless and will leave it penniless, if we have bread on the table and shoes on our feet, that's enough.

1 Timothy 6:7-8 MSG

Don't be obsessed with getting more material things. Be relaxed with what you have.

Hebrews 13:5 MSG

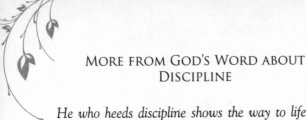

MORE FROM GOD'S WORD ABOUT DISCIPLINE

He who heeds discipline shows the way to life, but whoever ignores correction leads others astray.

Proverbs 10:17 NIV

Folly is loud; she is undisciplined and without knowledge.

Proverbs 9:13 NIV

Whoever gives heed to instruction prospers, and blessed is he that trusts in the Lord.

Proverbs 16:20 NIV

My son, do not despise the chastening of the Lord, nor be discouraged when you are rebuked by Him.

Hebrews 12:5 NKJV

No discipline seems pleasant at the time, but painful. Later on, however, it produces a harvest of righteousness and peace for those who have been trained by it.

Hebrews 12:11 NIV

MORE FROM GOD'S WORD ABOUT INTEGRITY

Till I die, I will not deny my integrity. I will maintain my righteousness and never let go of it; my conscience will not reproach me as long as I live.

Job 27:5-6 NIV

May integrity and uprightness protect me, because my hope is in you.

Psalm 25:21 NIV

In everything set them an example by doing what is good. In your teaching show integrity, seriousness and soundness of speech that cannot be condemned, so that those who oppose you may be ashamed because they have nothing bad to say about us.

Titus 2:7 NIV

A good name is to be chosen rather than great riches, loving favor rather than silver and gold.

Proverbs 22:1 NKJV

The integrity of the upright shall guide them....

Proverbs 11:3 KJV

More from God's Word about Miracles

I assure you: The one who believes in Me will also do the works that I do. And he will do even greater works than these, because I am going to the Father.

John 14:12 HCSB

But as it is written: "Eye has not seen, nor ear heard, nor have entered into the heart of man the things which God has prepared for those who love Him."

1 Corinthians 2:9 NKJV

For nothing will be impossible with God.

Luke 1:37 HCSB

You are the God who works wonders; You revealed Your strength among the peoples.

Psalm 77:14 HCSB

With God's power working in us, God can do much, much more than anything we can ask or imagine.

Ephesians 3:20 NCV

MORE FROM GOD'S WORD ABOUT KINDNESS

Finally, all of you be of one mind, having compassion for one another; love as brothers, be tenderhearted, be courteous.

1 Peter 3:8 NKJV

Love is patient; love is kind.

1 Corinthians 13:4 HCSB

And may the Lord make you increase and abound in love to one another and to all.

1 Thessalonians 3:12 NKJV

And be kind and compassionate to one another, forgiving one another, just as God also forgave you in Christ.

Ephesians 4:32 HCSB

Pure and undefiled religion before our God and Father is this: to look after orphans and widows in their distress and to keep oneself unstained by the world.

James 1:27 HCSB

MORE FROM GOD'S WORD ABOUT ETERNAL LIFE

Pursue righteousness, godliness, faith, love, endurance, and gentleness. Fight the good fight for the faith; take hold of eternal life, to which you were called and have made a good confession before many witnesses.

1 Timothy 6:11-12 HCSB

Jesus said to her, "I am the resurrection and the life. The one who believes in Me, even if he dies, will live. Everyone who lives and believes in Me will never die—ever. Do you believe this?"

John 11:25-26 HCSB

I have written these things to you who believe in the name of the Son of God, so that you may know that you have eternal life.

1 John 5:13 HCSB

And this is the will of Him who sent Me, that everyone who sees the Son and believes in Him may have everlasting life; and I will raise him up at the last day.

John 6:40 NKJV